You 53 Cost

A CLUELESS MAN'S GUIDE TO RELATIONSHIPS

*What Women Know Intuitively About Relationships—
But Men Have to Learn*

KELLY C. FISHER

Seven Pillars Press

Copyright © 2010 by Kelly C. Fisher.

All rights reserved. Printed in the United States of America. No part of this book may be copied or reproduced in any manner whatsoever without written permission except in the case of brief quotations embodied in critical articles or reviews. For information address Seven Pillars Press, LLC, 142 East Tenth Avenue, Anchorage, Alaska 99501

www.sevenpillarspress.com.

ISBN: 978-0-9841296-0-7

LCCN: 2009909886

Fisher, Kelly C. [1946 –]

A Clueless Man's Guide to Relationships: What Women Know Intuitively About Relationships—But Men Have to Learn / Kelly C. Fisher—1st ed.

10 9 8 7 6 5 4 3 2 1

Purchase this book at: **www.acluelessman.com**

*For Janet Lindeman, Ph.D.
who taught me how to learn*

CONTENTS

INTRODUCTION	1
THE SMART MAN PROBLEM	3
WHAT DO WOMEN WANT?	7
Loving Thoughts	8
Loving Actions	10
Collect Love Points	11
Who Is Your Partner?	14
That Inner Kid	16
Loving Versus Liking	18
Unexpected Responses	19
You May Get Picked On	20
BASIC COMMUNICATION	23
Communication 101	24
Women Interact	25
A Serious Warning	26
Talk About Feelings Because…	27
Mirroring	28
Body Language Shouts!	29
Attack and You Lose	31
Fight Fair	33
What Was Your Purpose in Making That Statement?	34
COMMUNICATION PITFALLS	37
Don't Say "But"	37
"Why?" Is Rude	38
Your Partner Doesn't "Need" to Do Anything	39
Talk Bad Not Care	40
Sarcasm Is for Snobs	40

Teasing	41
Being Right Is a Mistake	42
Don't Talk Nonsense	43
Rudeness	44
Who Is Responsible?	45
The 72-Hour Rule	45
Don't Fix Your Partner's Problems	47
Ask for Permission	48
Honesty Is a Necessity	49

COMMUNICATION SOLUTIONS	51
The Miraculous Results Formula	51
Who Wins?	54
Say You're Sorry	56
Children, Family, Friends, and Coworkers	57

FIX YOURSELF	59
You're Dumber Than You Think!	59
Resentments and Expectations	60
Clean It Yourself or Shut Up	62
Be Pleasant Doing Chores	63
Sex	64
A Nice Guy	65
Divorce	66

HELP YOUR PARTNER	69
Bad Presents	69
Needs vs. Wants	71
Reaffirm Your Partner	72
A Perfect Vacation	73
The Gift of Success	75
What If It Isn't Broken?	76
Important Rites of Passage	77
Commitment	79

LIFE IS GOOD	81
Good Luck	81
Perfection Is Relative	82
Assume the Best	83
Wife Whisperer	85

THE END? HARDLY!	87
ACKNOWLEDGEMENTS	89

INTRODUCTION

In an episode of the animated television series, *South Park*, the characters discover their underpants are going missing. Gnomes are sneaking into their homes at night and stealing them. The boys follow the gnomes to an underground cave and discover a huge pile of underpants, and when they ask the gnomes why they did it, their response is that stealing underpants is just Phase 1. They point to a large chart on the wall of the cave: Phase 1—Collect Underpants, Phase 2—?, Phase 3—Profit. When the boys ask the gnomes about Phase 2, they look confused and all they can do is repeat: Phase 1—Collect Underwear, Phase 3—Profit. The gnomes don't have a clue about Phase 2.

This is exactly how I used to approach relationships. Phase 1—Find Woman. Phase 2—? Phase 3—Happiness. I was, however, never getting the lasting happiness "profit" from any of my relationships. I was as clueless about the Phase 2 of relationships as the gnomes were about the Phase 2 of business. Phase 2 is the most important relationship phase of them all. While perfect happiness is not attainable, this book is a guide to help men get the most happiness possible out of a relationship.

I am not a psychologist. I am a lawyer who has been married four times. My training has been purely trial and error, the school of hard knocks combined with an unwillingness to give up on relationships. Applying these suggestions to my relationships has benefited me. I believe that they can improve your relationships, help you avoid some relationship problems, and get you out of other problems you will certainly find yourself in. None of us is perfect. Everybody has problems.

Don't worry if your story is so different from mine that we seem to have come from different planets. The people who taught me these rules and principles were often very different from me. The people I have passed them on to have often been equally different. In my experience, however, these suggestions are basic to the relationships between men and women regardless of our individual stories.

Whether a suggestion is scientifically accepted is irrelevant to me as long as it works. Let your own experience be your guide. A scientifically proven suggestion that doesn't help is worthless. An unsubstantiated suggestion that produces results is worth trying. Go for results, not validation.

I learned these lessons one at a time from many people over many years. By reading this book you can learn in several hours what it took me years, often painful ones, to learn. Now I usually know what is happening in my marriage, which has lasted almost fifteen years. I am confident that because of these relationship skills, the marriage will last the rest of my life.

There is no requirement to approach these suggestions in order. Depending on you and your relationship, some rules will be more important than others. Some principles will be more effective for your specific relationship problems and opportunities. You might start by reading the whole book through from front to back, so you will see what it contains. After that, you can skip from chapter to chapter, choosing the topics you think are most relevant at the moment. You could also read, consider, and apply one chapter at a time.

No matter how you approach them, you will find that the suggestions in this book are easy to learn and apply (once you develop the habit). However, you may also have an initial barrier to overcome. I call this barrier the "Smart Man Problem."

THE SMART MAN PROBLEM

Some men have what I call the "Smart Man Problem." I myself am a "Smart Man," which means that I thought I was smart enough to solve certain relationship problems that had plagued me for years—and refused to accept, in the face of repeated failures, that I was not smart enough to solve them after all. If you are a Smart Man too, and you have used your best thinking to solve your relationship problems, and those problems remain unsolved, then at some point you need to accept that you are just not smart enough to solve them on your own.

The solution to the problem is going to be either something you have already considered and rejected as wrong, or something you are not able to come up with on your own. In either case, you are going to need a little help. And, most importantly, the solution is likely to make no sense to you at all; otherwise you probably would have figured it out for yourself by now.

Speaking personally, there came a time in my life when I realized that if I wanted to learn to be connected to someone in particular—in this case my daughter—I was going to have to learn how to be connected to people in general. This was not what I had been hoping for, actually; years earlier, I had decided that I wanted out of human society. But when I finally realized that I really did belong here, I also realized that *I was going to have to figure out how to make it work.* As I tell people who are on their own roads to recovery, once you acknowledge that a problem exists, you are screwed. There is no going back from that first acknowledgment. You can no longer forget, or go back, and staying put won't heal the pain that drove you to try to avoid the problem in the first place. I had to do something. This knowledge was the beginning of a long journey through Smart Man territory, where my own initial efforts were successful—to a point.

When I realized that I was going to have to figure out how to become connected with people, I made some major changes in my life. First, I stopped drinking. Drinking had made my life worth living when I was younger. Eventually all it did was help me ignore my relationship problems, and left me pretty much absent in relationships. It also stunted my emotional growth, keeping me at the emotional level of a teenager. As if being a teenager isn't unfortunate enough, acting like one when I was in my thirties was unpleasant for me and everyone else. While I was drinking my mind was too cloudy, and my ability to follow through to any goal was too low. I wasn't able to make commitments because I didn't know who I was as an adult—I had to find out who I was. Then any changes I made would be based on the firm foundation of who I actually was, not who I imagined myself to be.

I started to see a therapist shortly before I quit drinking and I continued to see her on and off for several years. I still see her every year or two when she comes back to town. I like to check in and get her feedback on how I'm doing. She and I worked long and hard to get me to my goal of being as sane as an average person in all areas of my life. In that period I still went through two more marriages. Yet I was committed to improving myself, and willing, eventually, to accept I had hit the Smart Man Problem. She taught me many of the suggestions about relationships in this book.

If you are a Smart Man who has exhausted his own best effort to make changes, it stands to reason that any solution offered from outside will, at least right now, seem too simple, too silly, or just plain wrong. Results, however, should be your goal. Results are the only markers of success, even when the reason for each success makes no rational sense to you. The Smart Man has to accept his limitations, step into the unfamiliar, and hope for the best. Here is your chance to be really smart.

WHAT DO WOMEN WANT?

They want to know, without any doubt, that they are loved. It's as simple as that. Without some action on your part, however, your love is just an unshared state of mind and they won't know how you feel. "To love" someone requires action, not just thought. How you act to let your partner know she is loved is the most important skill you can have in a relationship. If you want your partner to know that you love her, you must take some action; you must do something that lets her know that you love her.

You can be madly in love with someone who will never know if you don't let her in on the secret—so you must say or do something to show her love. In my earlier marriages I told my wives that I loved them. But no matter how strongly I felt the love, I learned that simply saying "I love you" was not enough. What is crucial to showing love is to regularly say and do things that let your partner know that she is loved. The easiest way to do this is to simply say out loud, or <u>act on, every positive thought about her that comes to mind.</u>

• • •

This chapter will describe the techniques that make it easy to speak and act so that your partner knows you love her. Initially, they may seem simplistic—until you start to notice the results. The next three chapters will improve <u>communication</u>

between you and your partner—there really are simple rules that can make discussing difficult topics easier. The final three chapters suggest ways you can adjust your behavior so that your partner, and you, are happier.

Loving Thoughts

I was surprised to discover that I needed to learn how to regularly show love to my partner. I developed a rule to make it easy: <u>Every time I have a positive, loving thought about my partner, I say it out loud.</u> I try not to put any filters on saying positive things. If I think it and it's positive, I say it. Since I love my wife all the time, it is important for me to let her know that I love her all of the time. Saying "I love you" is always important, but if it were the only thing I ever said, even if I said it frequently, it wouldn't be enough. I would start to sound like a broken record—in short, somebody who was losing interest in her.

You may not like your partner all the time (every person has her moments) but let's assume in this chapter that your love for her is constant (<u>although it can vary in degree depending on your mood, which we'll talk about a bit later</u>). Where love is constant, day in and day out, hour upon hour, expressions of love should be constant, too—day in and day out, hour upon hour. You can love your partner with all your heart, but if you don't let her know, there is simply no other way by which she is going to know it. Every loving feeling and thought that you have about your partner that you don't say out loud or act on in some noticeable way *just won't count*.

It may seem that most women require more expressions of love than men do to feel loved. It is just as likely, however, that men are slacking off. Women are usually better at showing love than we are. We may not notice the consistent effort women are putting into their relationships with us because we have gotten used to being bathed in their constant affection. Either way, it doesn't matter who is different or who needs more;

what is important is that we each show all the love we are feeling for our partners, consistently and forever.

Initially, you will probably feel awkward, and perhaps embarrassed by saying all the positive thoughts that come to mind, at least until it becomes a habit. Any new behavior usually takes three weeks or more to become a habit. Stick out the awkwardness for three weeks! Then like any other habit it should become second-nature.

• • •

Everyone enjoys constant spontaneous reminders that he or she is loved. It makes us feel good, and it makes everybody's day go better. I tend to have my head in the clouds and focused on my own stuff much of the time. My wife likes a lot of attention. It is very important to our relationship that I keep the habit of telling her all my loving thoughts. Ten or twenty comments, or more, a day is not overdoing it. Some partners may not need as much attention to know they are loved, but let them tell you that you are doing enough or too much. I doubt that it will be the latter.

One of the things that helped me get past my concerns about saying too many loving things to my wife is the effect it has on her. She almost always notices and appreciates what I say. I have never been able to say and do so many loving things that she complains.

When you start telling your partner all your loving thoughts, the sudden increase (or even beginning?) of loving comments may take her by surprise. Even after four wives, I can't predict how any woman will react to change. My guess is that some will ask you what is going on. The best response is to say that you realized that you were thinking about her more often than you had been saying, and that you decided to start letting her know how often you thought about her. Don't ham it up. Just say what you feel.

A word of caution: Don't make up positive comments. False comments are easy to spot and body language that doesn't match the comment can give you away. False (untrue, insincere, or forced) positive comments can do serious harm by causing your partner to wonder why you need to make up positive things about your love for her. Nobody wants to wonder why she is being lied to, particularly about love; the answers are often unpleasant. Don't create that harmful situation. Saying whatever comes to mind naturally, right when it comes to your mind, will ring true.

Loving Actions

Spontaneous loving actions are just as important as loving words. Doing simple little things that let your partner know you love her can be tremendous fun—for both of you. I get a kick out of doing them, and my wife likes to know that I am thinking about her. Even when I miss the mark, I still get points for the effort. Get creative!

For example, I try to brush against my wife or reach out and touch her when I pass her. I open doors for her, pull out chairs, and do all of that kind of stuff; anything I can think of to act on my love for her. Sometimes I do unexpected chores or buy little treats for her. Once I got her a little mechanical something (a yellow bird with antlers and Christmas bells—you couldn't really tell what it was supposed to be) that sang and did the Macarena. She loved it and kept it until she passed it on to a neighbor kid who just had to have it.

I'm also the keeper of the chocolate, because she doesn't like it tempting her all of the time. Whenever she gets a craving I almost always have some chocolate hidden somewhere. And the few times I blew it, I went to the store to buy more right away—cheerfully, because I knew how much she would enjoy the chocolate.

You won't always know what to do. Learning takes time, like everything else; just try to hit on what works. For instance, I reach over and hold my wife's hand several times a day. How did I learn to do this? I held her hand for the first time in a restaurant on our first formal date; she looked a bit uncomfortable when I did, and only much later did she tell me that holding hands is very important to her—that it means love, caring, and commitment. Today, we hold hands often: when we watch a movie, when we drive somewhere, when we go for a walk. Some of our friends think it is all a bit much, but I like doing it, and to my wife it means LOVE in capital letters.

Always think about your actions, and what they might say. Pay more attention to your partner than you do to your pets (and your friends). If you get this hierarchy wrong, your partner will surely notice, even if the imbalance is small. For example, I had developed the habit of giving my friend's Akitas a full body massage each time I entered the house. Well, my wife got jealous of the attention I was paying to the dogs and wondered why I didn't always pay as much attention to her!

Each of us has things we like having done for us. Touching is an important one. My wife likes having her hand held and her face rubbed. I like having her head resting on my chest and any kind of touching on the tops of my toes. Go figure! These things just make us feel good, and the lesson here is simple: If you know of something that makes your partner feel good, do it. If you don't know, find out.

Collect Love Points

Men usually don't stay focused enough in a relationship—except when we are dating. When I need a little extra motivation in showing love to my wife, I think about the practice of saying and acting on all my loving thoughts as "collecting love points." This silly concept reminds me to stay focused on letting my wife know how much I think about her.

To collect love points, I assume that every time I say or do something loving for my wife that creates a positive reaction, I earn a love point. If I compliment her I get one love point. If I do an extra, unexpected chore I get one love point. If I bring her flowers, I get one love point. You get the idea. If I buy her a diamond ring, I get one love point.

Whoa! Wait a minute. Only one point? This last example is important because it is less of an exaggeration than you might think. It may seem unfair, but most women are not like most men when it comes to big gestures and gifts. For a man, the bigger the gift, the more love points. For a woman, no matter how big or small the gift or gesture, you usually get only one love point. Furthermore, unlike with men, love points for women—all points, no matter how great your effort—don't last very long. They usually fade within several hours or days. I think the reason for this is that big gestures don't demonstrate continuing love. Big gestures, just like small ones, fade away and must be followed by a continuous stream of displays of affection and love. It is important to earn love points as often as you can because of their short shelf life.

The short shelf life for love points is really a blessing in disguise. Your partner wants to know that she is loved. She also wants to know that you are thinking about her often and are interested enough to keep showing your love. When you voice or act on every positive thought or feeling immediately after thinking it, you create a constant stream of demonstrations of a simple fact: that you are thinking about her day in and day out. It creates a warm glow.

Be careful to avoid the mistake of believing that grand efforts can carry you through difficult times in a relationship. Every loving word or action, big or little, gets you one love point only. But while those single love points don't last long, a consistent track record of love points can create a cumulative glow that lasts longer than any individual point and can help carry you through rough seas.

While a diamond ring produces fewer points than you would like, it is the kind of gesture that can create additional points when she looks at it later on. When my wife asks if I really love her, a sign that she is feeling insecure in other areas of her life or that I could be doing more to show my love, I tell her yes, give her a hug or a kiss, and pay a little more attention to her right at that moment. I reach for her hand and adjust the diamond so that it faces straight up, and she is reminded that I love her. I also take her ring sometimes and clean it, and then put it back on her hand as I did when we were married. There are an infinite number of things that you can do. All you have to do is try out the different ideas that come to mind, and keep repeating the ones that please your partner.

• • •

Are you feeling uneasy about my mushiness yet? Do many of these suggestions sound downright silly? I hope so. Otherwise you would probably already be doing similar things yourself. Remember the "Smart Man Problem?" The goal is to show your partner love. If being mushy or silly is the price, pay it. My brand of loving comments and actions for my wife may not suit you or your partner, though—and that is why it is important to say and do the things that come to *your* mind. Your partner fell in love with you, so even though you may feel uncomfortable showing more love at first, you will only be acting more like the person she fell in love with. Remember, men are most focused when they're dating.

The most important thing that I have learned about relationships is the need for constant, obvious acknowledgments of affection. The solution is to give as many little—as well as medium and big—loving gestures as possible to keep your love points account full. Remember that the points are all the same size, and rapidly fade. Get as many of them as possible, as often as possible, simply by speaking or acting on every positive thought you have about your partner. This will change your relationship for the better.

And while you're practicing that, don't forget to *respond* to every positive comment and action from your partner. It doesn't have to be a return compliment, but it should be some kind of acknowledgment—a thank-you, a smile, a nod, anything that lets her know that you noticed. When my wife says, "You're the best," I usually respond that I am the "second best." She knows that I heard her and that I feel the same way about her.

Who Is Your Partner?

You know who she is by her name and her looks, but who is she beneath those superficial facts? Learn all you can about her. What gestures and words speak directly to her heart? For my wife, holding hands is special, and likewise, each woman has her own unique ideas about what she feels are loving words and actions. Each woman also has her own likes and dislikes, hopes and fears, strengths and weaknesses. Some of these are conscious, and some are unconscious. Whether your partner knows and can articulate all her beliefs about herself isn't important. What is important is that you learn as many of them as you can.

The more you know about your partner, the better job you can do when you show her your love. Fortunately, every woman has many words and actions that mean *love* to her; you will be amazed at how many you will find when you start to look. All you have to do is pay attention to clues from your partner, try things out, and see what works. I got lucky when I discovered early on that handholding is so important to my wife; when I first held her hand, she had to start considering me as a serious suitor, and when I hold her hand now she feels loved.

Since then I have learned many things about her that allow me to fine-tune the words and actions I use to express my love. Over time I believe you can learn to increase the amount of love you have for your partner simply by learning her preferences. The capacity for your love will actually grow, but only if you pay attention and consciously experiment. Because you want your partner to feel more loved and be happier (and if you don't, why are you reading this?), your job is to learn as many of the words and actions unique to her as you can that make her feel loved. You may already know a lot of them—but I'm suggesting that you work at expanding your repertoire of loving words and actions to get even better at it. Then continue to act on them each and every time they cross your mind.

There are potential pitfalls. If you try something new and don't get the result you want, don't get upset and certainly don't cop an attitude. Just try something else. You've got lots of time and there are many things to try. (You will find some great comments and actions simply by accident. Luck can be a great help, so pay attention and don't miss unexpected positive reactions.) The reason this is a pitfall is that getting upset in situations where you are trying to be loving can send confusing signals. If you continue to expect favorable responses in spite of reactions to the contrary, you are just wasting time and setting yourself up for frustration.

Besides, your partner really is unique. No one is a perfect match for your personal notion of how a woman is supposed to react to love. You shouldn't be using only the traditional words or actions for showing love anyway, unless of course they spring to mind. (Oh, and don't plan your spontaneity either! It won't ring true.) Basically, concentrate on finding out what works rather than continuing to do the things you think "should" work. Go for results. Even when you have no idea why what you are doing works, even if it makes no sense to you, continue to do it anyway—because it works!

For example, you could do a number of chores around the house, some expected and some unexpected. When I make coffee for my wife, Mary, she always responds as if I have gone above and beyond the call of duty and it brightens her entire day. All I did was make a damn cup of coffee! To her, for whatever reason, this ordinary act by me says LOVE.

You will probably discover that some of the things that work for your partner can become overworked. You will see this is happening when the same words or actions that worked in the past start to produce diminished returns or even start to create a negative reaction. You will need to learn the correct pacing for those. That said, however, I still believe that it is pretty much impossible to overdo loving words and actions, provided they come from your spontaneous loving thoughts.

That Inner Kid

I believe that each person has an emotional default age from which he or she acts in their unguarded moments, and which influences him or her in guarded moments. My father told me as much one day after he watched me in a somewhat strange encounter with one of his neighbors. I was in my mid-twenties, working on my car in his driveway on a hot day. I was wearing a pair of shorts, no shirt, and at the time I had a mustache. An elderly woman, who lived several houses away and whom I had never met, walked over to the driveway. She was dressed as if for a tea party. My father introduced us, and she said a few pleasantries, and then she reached up and touched my mustache. She said goodbye shortly thereafter and went back to her house. My father was unusually pleased; he said that while he knew her husband, a retired general, he had never seen the general's wife out in the neighborhood before, not once during the several years he had lived there. He then asked me if I knew what had just happened.

He said that she had seen me working in the driveway, fit and mustachioed, and I had reminded the sixteen-year-old girl that lived in her ancient body of something—perhaps her mustachioed, handsome, young second-lieutenant husband when he was in the cavalry in World War I, or maybe some other cherished memory from her youth. She had come out of her home so that her inner teenage girl could briefly touch that memory again. My father was happy that I was able to do that for her. He then told me that he believed most people have inner teenagers.

I think my dad, mostly through his observation of my mother, got it right. Each of us has an age at which we experience ourselves when we are not thinking about our actual age. For most of us—the general's wife, my mother, myself—it is the middle teenage years. I know that I have to constantly remind myself how old I am before any physical activity, and to be more mature in public situations. In general, a lot of the playfulness in people comes from their subconscious perception that they are still young.

Mary is particularly accomplished at her work and is excellent in social situations; when she is in a relaxed situation, however, she is even more open and playful than most people. It makes her a special person because her default age isn't in her teens, like most people, but is somewhere around seven or eight—the age when kids are bright, inquisitive, charming, and silly. I love that she adds lightness and happiness to our home. In my experience there are very few people who behave like her when they are relaxed and happy.

Whatever your partner's default age, it is an important part of who she is. You shouldn't ridicule that part because it is a part that can't be changed—although you can cause her to stop acting from her relaxed inner self, to her detriment. I have made that mistake several times. My mother used to sing to us when my brother, sister, and I were young. She was a poor singer, but she liked to sing. I ridiculed her singing and she stopped. Several years later while I was still a child I realized what I had done and asked her to sing again. But she never did. It makes me sad that I did that to her, to her inner teenager, and to me.

I also tried to control my first wife's behavior. I thought I knew best how she should be acting, and after several years of "advice," I had some success in changing her. It was a terrible mistake. The more she behaved as I thought I wanted her to, the more I didn't like the result!

To sum up, you can't change your partner's inner kid. If you try you will only cause damage to her and to your relationship. If her inner kid has some annoying quirks, they are a permanent part of who she is and just have to be accepted. Fortunately, most aspects of every person's inner kid are positive and fun-loving. It is where much of the best in each one of us resides, so don't risk damaging the greater good for the sake of a few minor childish irritations.

Loving Versus Liking

Loving someone is constant, until such time as it may end. Liking someone you love is situational. I love my wife always and almost always like her—but not always. She has a number of quirks that I accept, some annoying behaviors that I endure, and occasionally she will do something that causes me to not like her. But through all the quirks, behaviors, and things she does that are less-than-perfect, it is still appropriate for me to share my loving thoughts and actions—even when I am otherwise mad. It is probably even more important then.

Whatever you do, don't pout when you're upset. People pout when they want others to know they are angry, hurt, or disappointed. Their goal is often a misguided effort to hurt their partner by showing them just how bad they made them feel—which is childish. If you have a problem with something your partner is doing, deal with her directly. Don't add your dark mood to the situation. You can use "The Miraculous Results Formula," explained later, to communicate your concerns.

When my wife and I have an issue that is causing strain, I still make every effort to show her that I still love her. As I learned more relationship techniques, it became easier to separate "like" from "love" and easier to continue to show my love without feeling that I was also approving of the unwelcome behavior.

The more you are able to distinguish between your constant love and your temporary dislike for your partner, the easier it will be to continue to show her love while you address the cause of the dislike. Continuing to show love does not mean you approve of the behavior you dislike. The two are not related. When you separate the two it becomes easier to work on the problem because you will not be overreacting. Problems with, and dislike of, your partner are only temporary and can be fixed. Keep showing your love in all the areas where you still like her, so that you don't let your dislike affect the entire relationship.

Unexpected Responses

If you don't get the expected response to some of your loving words or actions—then, as I said, don't pout. Not every great idea will mean the same thing to your partner that it does to you. If you are tempted to think that she isn't noticing your efforts, you may feel resentful or unappreciated. You might even think, "Why bother?"

Don't get in a snit. Her reaction, or lack of reaction, is probably unintentional. If it were on purpose, she would also be giving you other indications that she has some issues with you.

Your partner gets to be herself. The words or actions that have no effect on her (no matter how loving and important they may be to others) just don't count. If you become focused on words and actions that "should" work for her, you will miss the boat. Your job is to find the words and actions that actually *do* work for her. To find the ones that speak uniquely to her, keep trying new words and actions. And, of course, ditch any that have a negative effect.

Negative responses usually come as a surprise because they are not the reaction you were hoping for—but cut her some slack. Negative reactions to what you and others may think are great words and actions are often caused by unpleasant associations from your partner's personal or family history. You will undoubtedly run into several of these, and I can't tell you what to look for beyond an unexpected negative response.

This is where learning who your partner is becomes important. When you find that one of your comments or actions causes a negative reaction, remember not to do it again. Your partner (like everyone else) has her own set of conscious and unconscious beliefs about what comments and actions show love. There is no right or wrong to her feelings. You just have to learn your partner's preferences and act accordingly.

If you find yourself collecting love points to "win" or are keeping score for some reason other than your partner's well-being, this is a sure sign that you feel short-changed in the relationship. Maybe you are suffering resentment caused by unsatisfied expectations. There are other suggestions coming up that can help.

If you run into a steady stream of negative reactions, however, you are dealing with something else entirely. If your relationship is long-term you may be facing a major problem or even a change of heart in your partner. It is time to ask, "Do we have a problem?" and find out what you are up against. Or, if your relationship is just beginning, you should ask yourself if you even want to be in a relationship with someone who is always negative. Relationships require work, usually fun work, but a relationship that starts as a chore is probably not going to improve.

You May Get Picked On

Each of my four wives has a quirk that surprised me, and that I am reluctant to attribute to women in general. But with four out of four, I feel I should warn you in case it happens to you. At some point in each of my relationships I was told that I needed to make improvements. And at least one time in each of my relationships, I put great effort into making the suggested improvements. After several months of effort, each of my wives expressed disappointment that I hadn't done anything, let alone changed. All that I had been doing, all the changes I had made, just hadn't registered with them. They only realized the extent of my efforts when I gave them specific examples of all the things I had done. I don't know why these otherwise intelligent women were so ignorant in this regard.

I have heard that when things start to get better in a relationship, they will appear to get worse for a while. The reason is that where there is little hope of improvement, a partner's expectations will remain low. But where there is evidence of improvement, a partner's expectations will increase and outpace your improvement, perhaps for quite a while. This will feel particularly unfair. Here you are, finally headed in the right direction, and you are being accused of doing nothing or even of getting worse!

All I can say is, "Hang in there." Consider your partner's reaction, or lack of reaction, as an indication that serious effort on your part is necessary and that you are actually having some success—although it sure won't feel that way. Remind your partner of your efforts in subsequent conversations. It will help both of you.

In most cases, any initial skeptical responses from your partner to your showing her more love should be minor and not last long. The benefits will show up soon, if not immediately, and will last a lifetime. Hang in there! It is worth the effort. All you have to do is speak or act on every positive, loving thought you have about your partner.

BASIC COMMUNICATION

Most communication in a relationship will be casual, light, playful, informative, or loving conversation. Some communication however, will be more serious.

Women seem to have the ability to out-talk men. And I've found, in all my years of serious relationship talks, that they sure have the ability to stay in a conversation long after it has exceeded my emotional comfort level. I don't know if their advantage is their skill with language, a better understanding of emotions, or just more time to formulate their thoughts on an issue, since men often delay talking about problems.

Men postpone serious thinking and talking about relationship problems more often than women do. This used to seem like a good strategy, at least to me. It seemed easier to avoid than confront a problem—right? Wrong! The problem doesn't go away, and your partner only becomes more upset that you are ignoring the problem. It also gives her more time to think about it and prepare to talk circles around you. The easiest course of action is the one that is the hardest to initiate. Bite the bullet and start talking about whatever is making either of you uncomfortable. You know it is going to happen anyway, so you might as well score some points, probably not love points, by initiating the conversation—and especially don't avoid it if she breaks the ice first.

To help you get through your relationship's more serious conversations, this chapter will offer some basic rules and techniques. In my experience these rules for serious talks between men and women are not always well understood by women, so you may even want to talk to your partner when times are *good*, to set guidelines for the inevitable tougher times.

Communication 101

There may be a basic difference between what men and women want to accomplish by conversing. Women don't talk about problems to solve them as much as to share their feelings about them. It is dangerous to miss this distinction. If you focus on solving the problem when your partner is more interested in having you understand what she is going through, you will miss an opportunity to make her feel more comfortable. Often your understanding is more important to her than having the problem solved. It is your relationship—the two of you in this together—that is most important to her.

Men want to focus on problem-solving, and if the problem can't be solved, they want to forget about it. Women accept that many of life's problems don't have easy solutions, or any solutions at all, and they are more interested in acknowledging both persons' feelings about these difficult situations. They want to empathize with the feelings and support their partner and be supported in their own disappointment or frustration. This approach can sound inconclusive, and you may be scratching your head and wondering, "Why bother?" But in fact, women's approach can actually solve problems in relationships more often than men's. And what do you have to lose in trying her approach? If the problem remains unresolved but your partner thinks it has been properly dealt with—great. End of story.

For the longest time when my wife came to me with a problem I felt like a failure if I couldn't solve it. Now, by just suppressing my problem-solving instincts and empathizing with her problems and concerns, I can make her happier. I no longer feel the pressure and responsibility to solve my wife's problems, because all I have to do is listen and understand how she is feeling. This is called "letting her vent." (It's a great service to provide anybody.)

If my wife asks for my help in finding a solution, then I am Johnny-on-the-spot. If I think I have a great solution, but she hasn't asked me for it yet, I will ask her if she would like any suggestions I might have for solving the problem. If the problem seems serious, and neither of us knows what to do, I will ask if she would like me to think about what might be done. In this way I show that I have listened, that I care, and that I am willing to do whatever I can to help if she would like me to. And if she declines, then I had better keep my mouth shut.

Women Interact

The difference between sexes is not a bad thing. Men and women have formed relationships forever, and it makes sense to parcel out survival skills between the two. Each can then focus on what he or she does best—from each according to his or her ability, to each according to his or her need. A problem arises, therefore, when one party doesn't honor, respect, and utilize the other's superior skills. Women are the guardians and the grease of relationships, and they understand more intuitively than we do that the connections between people are the essence of being human—that human relationships are really the only game in town.

Before my third marriage my father told me, "Women are almost always right and when they tell you to do something that you can't think of a strong reason not to, just do what they say." Well why not? They love us, they have our best interests at heart, and they are the relationship experts.

I believe women are better than men at nurturing relationships while at the same time doing the normal tasks of living. Men tend to do one or the other and often concentrate on tasks before relationships. Consequently, when women ignore us, we tend to get on with our tasks and spend little time thinking about why we are being ignored. When we ignore women, however, we create a problem.

One of the cruelest things you can do is to ignore your partner. It hurts her because she cannot use her innate talents and her superior relationship skills. It also hurts because the essence of a relationship is trust, and if either partner does not fully participate, you or she breaks the trust innate in the decision to share lives with each other.

• • •

If your partner is being unreasonably abusive, withdrawing temporarily will definitely get her attention; she will find herself at a loss because she has nothing to work with. It is never appropriate, however, to ignore anyone for long. If you are the one who has crossed over the verbal abuse line, she will be inclined to stay in the conversation longer (take more abuse) because she is more adept at dealing with intense emotions. That doesn't mean you should keep talking. If you are able to see what you are doing, stop, and then explain that you are excusing yourself from the conversation until you have calmed down.

A Serious Warning

Let me say this again. The worst thing you can do in a relationship is to withdraw and not participate. It is a serious breach of the trust implicit in all relationships. It is the nuclear option, with all the resulting toxic fallout. Use it with caution after you have explained to your partner what you are doing and why, and then only for a specific, limited amount of time. Other chapters will discuss appropriate times to temporarily withdraw, and techniques that make its limited use okay.

Talk About Feelings Because . . .

A problem is only a problem when someone's feelings are involved. If you feel neutral, there is no problem. Feelings are like an itch or an ache; you either have them or you don't. Feelings are never wrong. The cause of a feeling may be valid, based on misinformation, downright silly, or simply unknown—but you still have the feeling and it still affects you.

Whether you do or don't understand your partner's reasons for feeling the way she does, it is less than useless to argue that she doesn't or shouldn't feel that way. I repeat: Regardless of where it comes from, a feeling is always a feeling to the person experiencing it, even when the underlying reason for the feeling is based on a misunderstanding.

Men prefer to talk about their thoughts and about the facts, not their feelings. As a result, men start off with a handicap in any serious conversation. Women talk more about feelings simply because they know where the real problems lie. By talking about the *feelings* involved, rather than the thoughts and facts, you will focus on what is really bothering your partner—and can make some real progress.

• • •

Unlike feelings, facts can be wrong. If you start by talking about facts rather than feelings, you are starting from a potentially weak position because your facts may be wrong. If you talk about your feelings first, you can't be wrong. No one can deny your feelings. When you talk about how you feel you are sharing what is most important to a relationship, and providing an opportunity for each of you to understand what the other is going through. Both you and your partner are then in a better position to discuss the facts that have caused the negative feelings.

Your partner already knows that having correct facts is less important than resolving bad feelings. Since it is the feeling that needs to be fixed, you first need to know what feelings are involved. Then you will know what the real subject of the conversation is, and only then can you add facts and your thoughts to the discussion as needed. If you discover you are wrong about the facts, that acknowledgment alone may help solve the problem. While you may have to admit you were wrong, you will feel better if your new understanding helps end the bad feelings between you and your partner.

There is another problem with leading into a conversation with facts. You will have taken control of the conversation by steering it toward your view of the potentially blaming and shaming facts without first identifying the real issue—those damn feelings! Don't do it! Go for results rather than winning an argument. Your approach should *always* be this: "Damn the facts, who cares if anybody was right or wrong, what can we do to fix our feelings?"

Mirroring

Okay, you cleared the first hurdle and successfully led the argument with feelings rather than facts. What next? An excellent technique to use in serious communication is called *mirroring*. Mirroring is saying back to your partner, in condensed form, everything she has just said to you. This will accomplish two goals. First, it will prove that you are listening. Second, it will give your partner an opportunity to correct you if you have misunderstood what she has said. This second benefit will save you from discussing completely irrelevant topics and help keep your partner from thinking you are nuts. Remember to mirror back all the feelings that were related to you, as well as any facts. Feelings, remember, are the most important part of any serious discussion.

If the subject of the conversation is a real hot-button issue, it can help to set speaking guidelines. Guidelines can help limit anger and confusion. One I have used is taking turns speaking. One of you gets to speak for as long as he or she wants with no interruptions. Then the other person gets to speak as long as he or she wants with no interruptions, remembering to first mirror back what was heard and to ask if it was heard correctly. By taking uninterrupted turns, several good things are accomplished. It avoids talking over each other and missing something important. It reduces the urge and the opportunity to score verbal "gotchas" (see the section, "Talk Bad Not Care") that will only anger the other person and not move you toward the goal of the conversation: resolution. Anytime you make your partner angry (a feeling), that will become the new most important topic of conversation, and will sidetrack you both from the original issue.

Mirroring and uninterrupted talking ensures that both you and your partner have had your full say, and that you both have been clearly heard, if not yet fully understood. Understanding what someone is saying is not the same as agreeing with what they are saying. It is, however, the first step to any meaningful conversation. It then becomes easier to work on the problem because both of you understand clearly what the other person feels and thinks.

Body Language Shouts!

Body language is an often-unacknowledged part of a conversation. Failing to understand this fact can be a real problem, because it is usually the most truthful and important part of anything you and your partner say to each other. Wherever your body language conflicts with your spoken words, the body language almost always trumps the words.

Most of us learn body language as infants and toddlers before we learn a spoken language. As we come to rely more on a spoken language we tend to forget just how important and prevalent body language is. Body language is tricky, tricky stuff, and learning to read your and your partner's body language is a valuable relationship skill.

People form often-permanent opinions about others within the first few seconds of meeting them. It all comes from our subconscious perception of the person's body language. Some common examples of body language that will negate any words to the contrary include folded arms (indicating hurt or defensiveness), lowered eyelids (indicating disbelief or boredom), and shifting in your chair during your partner's turn to speak (indicating disagreement).

My third wife was fluent in body language. Her words were often irrelevant. Once I learned which "language" to listen to, we began to communicate much better. Unfortunately, when I learned to listen to her body language rather than her words, it became clear to me that we did not have the same expectations about our marriage.

Occasionally I could even identify a problem that concerned her before she spoke the first word about it. Her body language was "speaking" it clearly. When you sense that the problem your partner is talking about doesn't seem to be the one that is upsetting her, your intuition is probably reading her body language. Try to identify the unspoken communication and mirror it back to her. The technique can help both of you refocus and identify what the real problem is.

Occasionally, the best course of action in a serious conversation is to adopt a flat attitude. Go into a computer-like mode, keeping as much emotion and body activity out of your conversation as possible. Keep talking about the relevant feelings while trying to hold at bay the emotions that the conversation brings up. This can help you stay focused on the emotions while not being distracted by them. If your partner challenges you on your apparent lack of concern, just indicate that you are actually very concerned—so concerned that you are intentionally dampening your strong emotions about the issue so that you can give it your best, unclouded, dispassionate attention.

The blessing of body language is that, unless you are dealing with a particularly self-aware and manipulative person, it always tells the truth—and it always speaks to feelings rather than facts. If your partner just doesn't seem to be getting what you are saying, it might be because she is "hearing" your body language instead—there might be a disconnect between your words and your body language. Ask her what she is hearing you say, and you may learn what *you* really feel about the subject.

And don't forget: Body language is not only negative. There is just as much positive body language. Think of all the smiles, relaxed postures, and physical openness that we associate with good times. Body language is another great way of showing your partner love and earning loving points. It can also alert you that you are not in as much trouble as you feared. On those infrequent occasions when my wife feels compelled to call me an idiot, I can tell from her body language whether I am in the doghouse or she is just flirting.

Attack and You Lose

Attacks always preclude serious conversation. If you attack, the attack will become the primary topic, relegating the original topic to a distant second place. Now you have two issues to deal with where before you had only one—and you are definitely headed in the wrong direction.

Some people think that the best defense is a good offense. But you and your partner are on the same team. Furthermore, an overzealous reaction that misdirects the conversation will pique your partner's interest, and she'll want to know what caused you to overreact. An attack from you can be an admission that the initial issue is so sensitive or so close to something you don't want disclosed, that you would rather fight than discuss it. An attack can also be triggered by a related, or unrelated, resentment. (Resentments are discussed later.) If you never attack your partner in a conversation, the attack can never become the topic of the conversation and you will stay focused on the original topic being discussed.

If verbal attacks are common in your relationship check out *The Gentle Art of Verbal Self Defense* by Suzette Haden

Elgin, Ph.D. The book teaches how to deflect the eight most common kinds of verbal abuse, starting with "If you really loved me...." I have learned to apply the defenses described in the book to my benefit. Reading the book will also train your ear to hear your own forms of subtle verbal abuse, which is the first step in learning how to stop doing it. None of us is perfect.

There are some topics, and even words, that carry such a strong emotional charge that a person can't discuss them without feeling attacked. My wife is greatly upset by being called stupid, particularly when she really is being stupid. I suspect the word has unpleasant childhood associations. When she is being stupid I can say she is inane, silly, ridiculous, brain-dead, or just about anything else I want—just not stupid. Sometimes she calls herself stupid, but no one else can without hurting her feelings. In my case, anything that strikes me as even mild criticism of my daughter will make me angry. I think this comes from my lingering guilt about leaving her when she was little. I will listen politely, but you had better be very fair and very accurate if you mention anything other than praise. (Fortunately she turned out well!)

If you find it hard to resist hurting your partner with words, it is a sign that you have other ongoing resentments, perhaps even unrelated to any particular topic of discussion. Saying hurtful things to the people you love isn't right, and it certainly isn't showing love. Maybe you feel underappreciated, or consistently nagged, or guilty about something you have done. You may not even know what it is. The best thing is to find out what is really bothering you and work on it yourself. Otherwise you will continue to overreact to your partner's often-reasonable behavior.

You are the only one who can fix yourself. In my case, when I feel exasperated by someone who isn't overtly rude, I automatically assume the problem is mine until proven otherwise.

Fight Fair

My parents taught me not to inflict verbal wounds. We each know how to insult, offend, and hurt other people with words, even people we don't know. In relationships we learn things about our partners that gives us a unique ability to hurt them seriously. With the increased knowledge comes an increased responsibility to not use that knowledge to hurt. Stick to discussing your feelings and the facts that caused your feelings.

Our brains seem to recall negative comments much better than positive ones. This is yet another reason to act on every loving thought. Those continuous loving words and actions will dilute our more unfortunate comments. If you strike out at your partner with some nasty verbal abuse, you will only create an additional problem that will be difficult and time-consuming to fix. The more memorable or creative your nasty comment is, the longer the damage will last, and it may leave a permanent scar on the relationship. You can apologize, but the memory of what you said will stay. If you can't resist fighting, just remember the cost incurred will be additional hurt feelings, and your partner will then be less disposed to work with you to solve the problem.

• • •

No one needs to subject himself or herself to insults. If your partner is out of control and unable to converse reasonably, it is appropriate to say that you won't accept her behavior and will get back to her later. She of course, has the same right to walk away if you are the one who has come unglued. Or, if things aren't yet too far out of hand, you could ask what her purpose is in making her comments. This might focus her mind on the fact that she has strayed beyond productive conversation.

Remember that withdrawing from participating in the relationship is the nuclear option of last resort to be used only sparingly. If this becomes necessary, be clear to your partner why you are only taking a time-out and when you intend to start talking again.

What Was Your Purpose in Making That Statement?

Women are often better verbal sparrers than men. If a woman uses her verbal skill to hurt or abuse you, you have several options. You can take it and think of it as an indication of just how angry she is or how important the problem is to her. Or you can stop the conversation temporarily. If you do stop the conversation, suggest a time limit—several hours or a day later—when you want to take up the conversation again. Sometimes sleeping on it, or after a meal, or a workout, are good ideas for calming things down. You should know what works best for you and your partner. Remember, if either of you is hungry, angry, lonely, or tired you won't be at your best.

There is also a middle ground between taking the abuse and just walking away. Before the abusive comments become too much, too distracting, or too far off the point, you can ask, "What was your purpose in making that statement?" This has the dual advantage of either requiring your partner to own up to the fact that she is attacking you or giving her the opportunity to explain that you misunderstood (or that she was not articulate enough to say what she intended to say).

Don't accept a response that it was "just a comment." Nothing is ever "just a comment." Every comment is for a reason, and you are entitled to an explanation. If she insists that it was just a comment, however, let her know that you take the conversation seriously and ask that she not make comments irrelevant to the discussion.

• • •

I almost never want to have a serious conversation. I have learned, however, that it is almost always best to discuss serious issues as soon as possible. I have two exceptions. One is when I really am too tired or distracted to pay proper attention. Then I say so and pick another time in the near future to have the conversation. The other is when I am unsure how I feel about the problem, and need more time to think it through. Then I suggest another time in the near future to continue the conversation.

When I am particularly confused about what is going on, it helps me to write down everything that has happened and everything that is said. This helps keep me from thinking in circles. If I skip this step, I am likely to miss important parts of the issue because I am fixated on other parts. The writing doesn't have to be any more than a list or some simple notes to remind me of what I already know, what else I should be thinking about, and if I am missing any important information.

Postponing a conversation is not a good idea unless you can show that you understand the problem (or need more time to think about it) and there is a logical reason for delay. Be sure you know what the problem is before you ask for additional time. If your partner says that you are not making any sense, just agree and acknowledge that you really do need a little more time to think about what she has said before you can respond.

It is very important to keep your promise to get back to your partner at the time you specified, even if it is to say you still need a little more time. Don't leave her with the impression that you don't take the problem seriously.

• • •

Men have a tendency to avoid serious discussions, and these are simple rules that will make having those discussions easier and less confusing. Executing them efficiently without stubbing your toe is another matter, which the next chapter addresses.

COMMUNICATION PITFALLS

The basic rules for communication are fairly easy to understand and apply. But learning and applying them will not be enough to keep you out of trouble. There are also a number of communication pitfalls that can trip you up. Have you ever had a conversation that angered your partner for no known reason? If so, you probably stubbed your toe on one of these. Most of them are innate bad habits that we don't understand are offensive—and often don't even know we have. Consider each of the following pitfalls and train yourself to stop using the ones that apply to you.

Don't Say "But"

Do not dilute loving words or actions with criticism. This is a recipe for disaster, and sometimes even a form of verbal abuse. As I said before, your partner will remember the criticism and not the compliment. Worse, you will foster the perception that any positive comment may be the lead-in to a complaint—and you will be creating a flinch-factor.

The easiest way to make this mistake is by using the word "but." It negates everything that came before "but" in a sentence. Think about it. If you say, "I really love you, but..." the message that comes across is "I don't love you because...."

The better word is "and." It's an inclusive word. It means that you believe both of the things you are saying. Although I think it is a mistake to put loving words and criticisms in the same sentence—maybe even in the same paragraph—you can always say "I love you and…" so as not to deny the love.

Substituting "and" for "but" takes some practice, because when you first start to make the change you will see how you really were negating (or at least weakening) whatever you said that came before the "but." What may be more difficult to digest is that your partner was certainly picking up on the inherent negation long before you were. She will be happy with the change.

"Why?" Is Rude

The five standard questions are "Who?" "What?" "Where?" "When?" and "Why?"

"Why" is the problem question for two reasons. First, it is often irrelevant. Remember, the most important issue is the feelings, not the facts. To focus on "why" is to turn the conversation back to the facts. Second, "why" is almost always an accusatory and confrontational question, and it carries with it the likelihood of proving someone was wrong. People usually ask "why" in a personal conversation when they want to blame someone. "Why did you wreck the car?" assumes fault. "How did the accident happen?" is neutral. "Why were you late?" assumes fault. "What happened to you?" is more neutral. "Why don't we have any fun anymore?" could be an attack, unless it is a question asked in all seriousness.

This tip is a simple one to implement. All you have to do is avoid "why?" and substitute "how?"—or else be sure that you are only after necessary facts, and are not trying to shame or blame your partner.

Your Partner Doesn't "Need" to Do Anything

No one likes to be dictated to or told what he or she has to do. Don't shoot yourself in the foot and start a fight by telling your partner she needs to do something. Saying, "Honey, you need to calm down," or "Sweetie, you need to be more reasonable," will get you in trouble. Statements like these make you the pompous know-it-all-in-charge and she the party at fault. Even if she is at fault, you gain nothing by pointing it out. Instead, say, "You seem quite upset," or "I feel you are being unreasonable." You will still have to deal with the issue that is bothering her, but at least you will be talking about how you feel and about your concern for her well-being, and not saying that her behavior is wrong.

• • •

There are many triggers that can set people off. Each of us usually has half-a-dozen or so. When my daughter has difficulty understanding something her husband is explaining and he says, "Look, this is easy," she doesn't hear what I think he means—"I know you can do this." She hears, "You must be stupid if you can't get this." When my wife is assisting me with a computer problem and she leans in too close, her body language makes me feel like a child who needs to be moved out of the way before causing further harm.

When you get a negative response to what you thought was encouragement, you have hit one of your partner's triggers. Stop using the offending phrase or body language in that situation. For instance, my son-in-law was confused until he understood that his intended encouragement actually felt like an insult to my daughter. And now when my wife helps me on the computer she stands back or suggests that she might understand the problem better if she could sit at the computer for a minute.

Talk Bad Not Care

As a lawyer I have often been recorded when I was speaking under stress in court. Until I heard the tape or read the transcript of what I said, I was always sure I had done a better job than I actually had. If you could hear a recording of yourself speaking in a stressful situation just once, you would probably never pick on anyone else's speaking ability again.

Don't let bad grammar, disjointed thoughts, bad analogies, or any of your partner's speaking quirks distract you from hearing the message she wants you to hear. The rhetorical quality of that message should be irrelevant. If your goal is to fight, fighting will be easy enough to do. But if your goal is to find out what the problem is, how your partner feels about it, and what if anything the two of you can do about it, then you must resist making easy, but irrelevant, criticisms about your partner's choice of words. Everyone's grammar, syntax, and thought processes suffer when he or she is upset. Don't take advantage of your partner's weakness.

Sarcasm Is for Snobs

I have a friend who was having problems with his wife, his business partner, and other people as well—including me. When he finally came to me for advice about his relationships, I suggested that he stop being sarcastic. At first he denied it. I gave him a few examples. Then he remembered several other instances where he had used sarcasm. But he still didn't see sarcasm as a problem. He was proud of his creativity and his concern about "helping other people." I explained my belief that sarcasm was for snobs who thought they were better than the rest of us and who were using their superior intellect to be clever and criticize people, thus avoiding honest, direct communication about what was really bothering them. That caught his attention.

I don't know if sarcasm is a form of verbal abuse, but it sure is annoying. It is also counterproductive. Nobody likes to be the recipient of sarcasm. It is just criticism done up clever, and nobody likes people being clever at his or her expense. The natural reaction is, "The sarcastic SOB is not only criticizing and correcting me—he is showing off, too." You might as well just admit you're an insensitive dolt, because everybody else has already pigeonholed you.

The problem with sarcasm is that it is a blunt tool in your communication repertoire, and it damages relationships. Unfortunately, people who are sarcastic often think that they are being kind to the recipient of their often-unsolicited advice. This makes it harder for the sarcastic person to see that he or she is being rude. If in doubt, ask a friend, a true friend, if you are sarcastic. Or ask your partner. Then cut it out if the answer is yes.

My friend agreed to stop being sarcastic for a week and report back. Every aspect of his life and his relationships got better. He found that people were less resistant to his direct advice than they were to his sarcastic advice. He became happier, too, and he didn't miss his sarcasm. So, the moral of this story is "don't shoot yourself in the foot." Make a change if you have to, and go for positive results.

Teasing

Teasing is a wonderful way to become more intimate with someone. It can be a form of flattery—fun and intimate and bonding, a good way to show love. You can't effectively tease your partner, however, unless you understand her.

Unfortunately, teasing is often used as an indirect way to express anger. Cruel teasing is usually caused by resentment when something isn't going your way, perhaps for a long time. In this case teasing is often a form of revenge, and it sends mixed messages of love and disapproval.

Here's a good rule of thumb: if you find yourself saying, "I was just teasing," you have gone too far. Identify the source of your anger and resolve it. Don't continue to tease your partner excessively and inappropriately—because if you have to make an excuse for your teasing, then there is no excuse for it.

But don't shy away from teasing in general. Couples who are more creative at light, loving teasing are happier, have more fun, and are better able to weather the rough spots in their relationship. Appropriate teasing is just another form of acting on your positive loving thoughts.

Being Right Is a Mistake

Two words about being right: avoid it. In a relationship, being right is highly overrated. It's not that the "right" answer is necessarily irrelevant. It's just that the right answer may be irrelevant to the situation at hand. The goal in a relationship is to feel good and have your partner feel good, not be right for the sake of being right.

Being right often means that your partner is wrong. Is it important enough to point that out? If being right makes either of you feel worse, why go there? This is not to say that there are no things in a relationship more important than good feelings: finances and proper care of children are some examples of things that matter a great deal and are definitely right or wrong. These topics need to be addressed politely, regardless of either partner's feelings.

I believe my wife is wrong about some political issues, doctors, some nutrition fads, and how to prune shrubs and trees. It doesn't matter, though. We have discussed each and I am not going to change her opinion because of course she believes I am the one who is wrong. She is frequently wrong about less important things, too, like where the remote is, whether she will need a coat, and how long it will take to finish a given chore, but why should I care? She loves me and she does everything in her power to make me happy. If I focus on, or comment on, the right or wrong of any of these inconsequential issues, I diminish our happiness.

I think it would be rude of me to point out what I see as errors when she is otherwise perfect. Particularly since I have my own vast inventory of deficiencies. I can't, for instance, find anything even if it is right in front of me. If it isn't where I expect it to be, it simply becomes invisible. I tend to focus on the exact meaning of words spoken to me, often missing the intent of the speaker. My tolerance for computer problems is so low that I won't turn my computer on for days. If always being right were a requirement for a happy relationship, I would be living alone.

Since being right is usually unrelated to happiness in a relationship, it is counter-productive to point out that your partner is wrong. Once you are right, for no good reason other than to prove you are somehow better than your partner, what have you got? A hollow victory and an unhappy partner!

Don't Talk Nonsense

My father taught me that if you don't know what to say, it is better to say nothing at all. He wasn't speaking about intimate relationships, but his advice can keep serious conversations focused. If you make stuff up, guess, or lie, you are no longer dealing with the real situation. If you try to create a diversion to avoid or smooth over a problem, you are not solving the problem—you are shooting yourself in the foot. When the stuff you made up is discovered, you will have to deal with your partner about your deception.

If you need time to think, take it. It is okay to say you don't have a clue as to what is going on. The important thing is to let your partner know you are listening to what she is saying, and that you are confused and need more clarity. If you are too upset at the moment to think clearly, take the time to calm down. Just tell her what you are doing so that it doesn't look like you are ignoring the problem, ignoring what she said, or ignoring her.

The most common mistake is to offer an explanation that isn't directly related to the problem. If, for instance, tardiness is your problem, you have been late once again, and your partner complains, the reason you were late this time (even if valid) is not relevant to your usual rude behavior. Offering an excuse, even a legitimate one for your latest tardiness, is only avoiding the real topic of discussion. Your partner will know you just got lucky and are dodging discussion of the problem again.

Rudeness

I think that rudeness is the most common human sin. I don't understand the need to make oneself feel better by making someone else feel worse. When a person is rude to me I ignore their message. The reason is simple: I don't value that person's opinion. All I care about is the manner in which people let me know what they think.

But when a partner is rude the message can't be ignored. I value my wife's opinion and she values mine. When I am rude to her it is almost always because there is something bothering me that I am not addressing directly. Just as with pouting, I am showing displeasure without identifying the problem. If you find yourself being rude, look for the underlying problem and deal with it directly.

Each of us can be continuously, often inadvertently, rude in minor and occasionally major ways—playing the TV too loudly, leaving the toilet seat up, tracking in dirt, forgetting to say we are going out. The list can be endless. No one is perfect. So, after situations where you have been even slightly rude, it is important to say that you are sorry.

When my wife used to act in a particular kind of rude way I eventually learned that she was actually depressed because she was thinking about her brother who was terminally ill with cancer. It was almost always the case that she had talked to her brother or a family member earlier in the day. Once I discovered this connection, I stopped feeling put-upon by her rudeness and started to give her more tender loving care when I found her in that mood. The problem was solved because, once I understood what was happening, there was no problem—just another opportunity for me to prove I loved her and was there for her.

• • •

It is equally important to avoid being rude to other family members because there is no avoiding them. And when family and friends are rude to me I give them more latitude. Usually they are just being a typical, imperfect person. I also pay a little more attention in case the rudeness stems from an underlying problem. If I can't figure it out I ask a question like, "Are we okay?" or "What's going on?"

Who Is Responsible?

Almost nothing is entirely your fault. Don't let your partner convince you otherwise, because it's a trap. Your partner bears some degree of responsibility in almost every situation. To assume, or be convinced, that you are entirely at fault is to accept that your partner is not mature enough or adult enough to be responsible for her own actions and decisions. Even if she doesn't understand this mistaken message on a conscious level, it will certainly come through on a subconscious level and she will think less of you for the insult to her free will and personal responsibility. Therefore, don't treat your partner like an immature bimbo, even if she demands that you do.

Conversely, nothing is entirely her fault. Individual acts may be entirely the fault of one person or another, but a problem with the relationship belongs in varying degrees to both of you.

The 72-Hour Rule

The "72-Hour Rule" is a gross approximation of an important concept. Roughly stated, when a man has a physical, visceral reaction to a relationship event (such as when he gets mad, hurt, or shocked) it generally takes him 72 hours to calm down enough to think clearly about the situation again without being clouded by his emotions. For a woman the recovery time is about 11 hours.

These numbers are variable and some men can recover faster than some women, although men typically take longer to recover than women. That being said, consider the effect of the different recovery times. When a woman has recovered 11 hours after a fight and the man remains upset, he will wonder why she is pretending that everything is back to normal when it most obviously is not. When a woman, having recovered, looks at the man who is still suffering, she will wonder why this jerk is holding onto his angst longer than necessary when any normal person would have gotten over it by now. Each is angry with the other because neither understands that each person requires a different amount of time to recover from emotional shocks. Understanding this difference will help you each get off the other's case, and allow both of you to heal before re-engaging in a conversation. Restarting the conversation too early, before each person has fully recovered, is a mistake because emotional stress diminishes your ability to focus on a problem, and you will be more sensitive to additional hurt.

Accepting the 72-Hour Rule has allowed me, over time, to bring my recovery time down to hours rather than days. I have the advantage of being able to reasonably assume that my wife does not intend any harm, and I feel safe sticking my head back out earlier—which is fortunate, because she thinks the whole 72-Hour Rule concept is bunk.

• • •

I am not citing any authority to substantiate the 72-Hour Rule, or any of the other rules I refer to. A scientifically proven rule that doesn't help you is worthless. All I care about is whether a rule, as a working principle, improves my relationship. By accepting the 72-Hour Rule I can avoid conversations when one of us is too upset to talk. Let your own experience be your guide as to whether any of these rules and principles in this book help you.

Don't Fix Your Partner's Problems

Do not try to fix your partner's problems unless she asks for your help or advice. You have enough of your own problems to keep you occupied.

When she tells you about a problem, she is not asking you to fix it. She is letting you know what she is going through and looking for acknowledgement, acceptance, and empathy. An appropriate response to everything from a simple whinge to a lengthy tirade is something like, "I hear you. That really sucks. I can see why you feel that way." And you might finish with, "If there is anything I can do to help …?"—but not every time.

Wait for your partner to ask for advice. If she doesn't want advice, and you can't stand to watch her suffer, leave—after you have acknowledged her feelings and the conversation is over. Intervene if she is about to hurt herself or damage something. If she complains, just say that you weren't paying close enough attention but you became concerned that she might hurt herself.

Don't tell someone how to do something, either. It puts you in the position of being a know-it-all, and this is not how you score love points. It annoys the hell out of me when I am doing household chores and my wife tells me I should be doing them a different way. Here is an example—and my solution. When she cleans the kitchen floor she gets out a mop and a bucket. She mops with soapy water. She mops with clean water. She lets the floor dry. Twenty minutes later she is done. When I clean the kitchen floor (it is only five by eleven feet) I get Windex and paper towels. I start at one end and work to the other in several minutes. When I am done the floor is squeaky clean and already dry—and she still thinks I'm the one who is nuts! My solution is that I don't clean the kitchen floor when my wife is around. She is happy when she sees that the floor has been cleaned. She knows how I did it, but she wasn't present and didn't feel compelled, for whatever reason, to "correct" me. Problem solved.

It is hard not to offer advice when you are sure your way of doing something is better. But resist the urge. There is simply no reason to offer unsolicited advice when your partner's way gets the job done. When, however, you can teach your partner a completely new way of doing something that will save her time or avoid injury, then you should speak. When my wife was stripping windows prior to repainting our house using chemicals that bothered her, I said, "You know, a heat gun might loosen that paint just as well. I know where I can borrow one if you want to give it a try."

And sometimes the easiest way to do something isn't the best way. I wash the kitchen floor the way I do in part because I don't like mops. I used them when I was in the army and in moonlighting jobs when I was in college, and I will be happier if I never see one again.

Ask for Permission

If you feel you really do have valuable advice, you can ask for permission to give it. You can also ask for permission to comment on or revisit a situation in the future. Either strategy has the advantage of indicating that you are paying attention. If permission is denied, however, you should keep mum. If you want to make corrections to your partner's knowledge of a situation, make them, but don't expect it to automatically change the situation. What affects your partner's emotions, what she feels, won't always be affected by corrected facts, at least not immediately.

I find it helpful when my wife and I, or even a friend and I, have grown tired of talking about some difficult issue, to ask for permission to bring the subject up again another time.

Then when you do bring it up your partner can't accuse you of dwelling on something she may not want to talk about—she has already agreed to talk again.

Occasionally, I comment even when I know my wife doesn't want advice. I limit myself to situations where I will feel worse about myself if I don't comment, than I will if my comment offends her. I have to believe that my advice is *that* important to her—if I think I can protect her from harm, keep her from making a big mistake, or solve a larger problem she hasn't yet realized exists.

You will learn by trial and error when and how to offer advice. Often it isn't necessary. And if you don't do it often, she will pay more attention to the times you do.

Honesty Is a Necessity

You have to be honest with your partner. I'm not talking about exhaustive honesty. That just gets burdensome and boring. You need to be honest about the important things, the ones on which people base relationships. If you are not honest about them, it will lead to problems.

Hard as it may seem at the time, honest discussion, as soon as possible, is always the easiest way out. If you are not honest, there is no good way to address the underlying problem. All you will have done is divert the discussion to a lie. When your lie is discovered you will have more problems: the fact that you lied, added to the existing problem you were trying to avoid. You will also have proven your lack of trustworthiness, which will make solving the two problems more difficult.

I have a personal exception to my own honesty policy, and now I pass it on to you. I never comment on my wife's weight. If pressed with the question anything like, "Do you think I look too heavy?" I respond, "You look fine to me," or, "I like you just the way you are," or something similar. I try never to pick at her with my "honesty" as a way to tell her I disapprove of something. I don't even do it in response to a direct question. She knows what her weight is and how she looks. She is just asking for acceptance.

Before we met she suffered an injury whose scar is easily covered by clothing. I am lucky enough to see her without her clothes, and her imperfection has never bothered me. She knows this from my words, my actions, and my body language. I think her injury is unfortunate, but it doesn't affect my love for her at all. So, when she feels insecure and asks for my approval and acceptance with a dangerous question, I respond that I like her just the way she is. Somewhere in the back of her mind she remembers that I originally accepted her, flaws and all, that she is wearing the diamond ring that I gave her, and that I stayed fifteen years in our marriage and have done my best every day to remind her that she is the one for me.

• • •

Avoiding communication pitfalls can dramatically improve your relationship with your partner. Whether you know it or not, most of the pitfalls mentioned in this chapter are either ineffective attempts to avoid serious communication or simply bad manners. Either will be pretty obvious to your partner. Avoiding these pitfalls can result in more focused conversations that take less time and less effort, and which actually resolve problems. The following chapter describes techniques you can use to resolve disputes fairly.

COMMUNICATION SOLUTIONS

The goal of all serious conversation is to make both partners happy. Basic communication skills will get you started. Avoiding pitfalls will keep you focused. The following suggestions will show you how to achieve a fair resolution. By putting these and the preceding techniques to use, you can get back to enjoying the happier parts of a long-term relationship.

The Miraculous Results Formula

It is best to talk about a problem sooner rather than later—as soon as you understand what is going on. In fact, even if you don't have a clue what is going on, it is a good idea to tell your partner that you think something is out of sorts (with you, not her!) but you're just not sure what it is. There is a good chance she may already have some ideas.

When you do understand what is going on, the Miraculous Results Formula is one of the best ways to talk about your concerns. It works when you are angry with your partner, when you want to change her behavior, and when addressing touchy issues. I learned it from my therapist as the "Anger Formula," but it works wonders in so many situations that I now call it miraculous.

When you are emotionally invested in a particular outcome, it is too easy for your feelings to dominate and obscure the subject of the conversation. This can make it difficult if not impossible to talk about the real problem. Without some way to get past the emotions, you risk a fight. Without some way to present your concerns dispassionately, you risk accusing or blaming your partner, and then two things will happen simultaneously: the blame will become the main topic of the conversation, and your partner will become defensive. The Miraculous Results Formula allows communication while bypassing your emotions and avoiding your partner's defensiveness. It's a pretty neat four-step trick.

1. Identify the problem behavior or situation that is bothering you, sticking to just the bare facts. This is an exception to the rule about talking about feelings first, and is okay because you will talk about feelings immediately afterwards, in Step 2. Do not deviate from or elaborate on those bare facts. You want to focus attention on the issue as narrowly as possible. For instance, say: "When you ⎯⎯⎯⎯⎯⎯⎯" and then fill in the blank with the offending behavior. Stay as focused as possible. For instance: "When you tell me how to wash the floor…" or "When you vacuum while I am napping…" or "When you mention that my best friend has a drinking problem…" or "When you refuse to talk to me about [a specific topic]…." DO NOT use the word "always" as in, "When you always…" or any other word that implies fault or blame. Never exaggerate!

2. Describe the feelings that your partner's behavior causes. Identifying the feelings is most important. Those feelings are the real reason for the conversation. If your feelings weren't hurt, if you weren't angry, upset, or concerned, there would be nothing to discuss. Understanding the facts is just a means to that end. You will engage your partner's attention when you describe how you are feeling. For instance, you can say, "When you ⎯⎯⎯⎯⎯⎯⎯, I feel ⎯⎯⎯⎯⎯⎯⎯" and then fill in the second blank with your feelings. "When you tell me how to wash the floor, I feel confused and hurt that you think I don't know how to do it well." Or, "When you mention that my best friend has a drinking problem I feel angry when I am reminded that I can't seem to figure out how to help him." Now the problem has been clearly laid out: this is your action and this is how it affects me and makes me feel—all very neutral, clear, and honest.

3. **Identify the action (or inaction) you would like your partner to take** so that you don't have to feel this way again. Say: "What I would like from you so that I don't have to feel this way (confused, hurt, sad, angry) is _____" and fill in the third blank with your suggested remedy. For example, "What I would like from you so that I won't continue to feel confused and hurt, is for you to accept that this is the way I like to wash the floor." Or, "What I would like from you so that I don't feel angry about what I can't do, is for you to understand that I worry about my friend's drinking every day and it upsets me when I am reminded that I haven't been able to do anything about his problem."

Notice that each one of these examples stems from resentment—resentment that your way of washing the floor isn't good enough and that you aren't being appreciated for doing it. Resentment because she hasn't paid enough attention to your concern for your best friend, and so forth. Once you've aired your resentment in this way, now it is time for the fourth, and hardest, step.

4. **Do nothing else.** Just wait. Don't ask for a response. Don't say anything else unless asked a question. Just keep waiting, and get on with your day. You could wait minutes, hours, or days for a response, and you may never get one. Many times, however, at some point you will notice that your partner has started to do what you want. It may seem like a miracle but it is simply the result of clear communication unclouded by blame or demands.

Assume your partner really does have your best interests at heart. It is amazing how clueless we all are at times. Because you are not blaming your partner, because you choose to trust that she is not hurting you intentionally, she doesn't need to feel ashamed or bad about her behavior. Since she doesn't have to deal with those feelings, she can focus on your real message. With this approach you have assumed correctly that she is not a mind-reader. You have given her information that some of her behavior bothers you on the assumption that she would want to know so that she could change. You have given her the benefit of the doubt that she just didn't know how her behavior affected you. Whether you think she should have known better is irrelevant to your goal of getting her to change her behavior.

Equally important, you have not made any demands on your partner. Demands can create resistance. You are simply telling your partner that something she is doing, or not doing, is making you feel bad and she now knows what she can do to fix it. That is why in many instances she just stops the behavior. Problem solved. No fight. No accusations. No blame. But if after a few days you don't get any results, and the unwanted behavior continues, bring the topic up again and this time ask to talk about it. Don't be upset if she doesn't remember your previous conversation. It probably means it was not an important issue for her. The good news is that if it is that unimportant to her, she should be less resistant to changing her behavior.

Who Wins?

I learned from my parents how to decide who wins when someone must win an argument. They said when there is an irreconcilable dispute, the one who feels strongest about the issue should win. It's only fair. Relationships require give and take, and there are times when giving isn't going to be easy. When, however, getting your way will cause more discomfort to your partner than giving up something does to you, then giving it up is the right thing to do.

When I married Mary, I had a handgun and a shotgun. She is very anti-handgun, but doesn't feel that strongly about shotguns. I like handguns, but not as much as I love my shotgun. So I sold the handgun (and spent the money to buy myself another toy—fair is fair) and kept my shotgun. We are both happy enough.

A dispute might be about anything: where to eat out, how to dress for a party, or what color quilt to get for the bed. These are the easy ones. There have also been several tougher ones that my wife and I have had to deal with. One of them was what to do about my daughter when she was finishing her second year of college with no credits earned toward a degree. I won this one simply because I couldn't let go or listen to reason. Mary knew that it would be too damaging to our marriage if she stayed involved. Fortunately, I figured out a way to motivate my daughter; and she went on to get A's and a master's degree.

It is important to let your partner know how important something is to you. When I want a new computer or camera, and my wife thinks it is unnecessary, my arguing its practical points usually results in a rebuttal. She thinks I am bouncing ideas off her and she is trying to be helpful with my decision-making process. Once, in exasperation, after losing another practical discussion about a laptop computer I wanted, I threw up my hands and said, "It's just a toy!" (probably a lot of truth there). Her response was, "Oh, well, if you want it, dear, you should go buy it." What happened!?

What happened was she realized that I wasn't really engaging her in a discussion about practicality. I was indirectly asking for her permission, or at least acceptance, in my buying it. As soon as she realized it was a toy that I really wanted, she understood that she could make me feel good by telling me to go ahead and buy it—and I try hard to not abuse her love by buying too many toys this way.

Say You're Sorry

Men seem to have a hard time saying that they are sorry. This is unfortunate because apologies are one of the most effective tools for calming or avoiding relationship turmoil. Apologies are simple to make and incredibly effective. Learning to apologize for your mistakes, both big and small, will improve your relationships immeasurably.

Saying you are sorry accomplishes many favorable goals. It is sort of like relationship grease. Apply it regularly and things will go more smoothly. Every one of us is constantly making mistakes. It's really no big deal. What is a big deal is making a mistake and not acknowledging it. It's not like your partner hasn't noticed or won't find out. By apologizing you let her know that you know that you screwed up. This keeps her from having to decide whether you are just an insensitive clod or actually intended to do the wrong thing. Even if she hasn't noticed your error yet, it is nice to clear the air before she does and it becomes an issue. Also, failing to apologize when you are wrong is an additional mistake that can hurt your partner, so an immediate apology can smooth over a mistake and allow you both to get on with the day.

We all can use a little forgiveness and understanding after making a mistake. By owning up to our mistakes early, we can lessen any negative feelings we caused. An immediate apology might enlist the help of your partner in minimizing the impact of whatever it is that we have done. Furthermore, since your partner is the person most affected, it is only polite to give her the opportunity to have an input if the situation needs to be corrected. It also helps to try not to do whatever you did again. This is key—try not to make the same mistake again.

• • •

Acknowledging errors and saying you are sorry works wonders with children, family members, friends, and coworkers too. Children are always screwing up as they learn how to do things and become socialized adult human beings. It is nice for them to see that they are not the only ones who make mistakes. It is also nice to show them how to handle mistakes—by apologizing and fixing the problem.

Apologizing to your friends and family members is important because the closer the emotional relationship, the more important acknowledging mistakes and making amends become. There is comfort created in important relationships when others know that they can rely on you to own up to your mistakes consistently and early. You create comfort by demonstrating that they are not going to find out about your mistake some other way, and then have the added burden of having to confront you about it.

And by the way, you only need to apologize for your actions or inactions, not your thoughts. If you are like me you have a lot of crazy thoughts. (I hope everybody does.) It is only when you act on inappropriate thoughts, usually by what you say, that they have an effect on others. It is only the words and actions that require apology, and obligate me to help fix the hurt feelings or mistake, and try not to repeat the error in the future.

Children, Family, Friends, and Coworkers

Most of the rules and principles discussed in this book work equally well on children, family members, friends, coworkers, and even the people you wouldn't necessarily associate with by choice. For instance, it is important to regularly and consistently let your children know how often you think positively about them. And like a romantic relationship, your relationships with friends and coworkers can benefit from the insights and skills this book provides; even if a relationship is a bad one, this book can help you to identify what is wrong and help you decide if it's best to separate yourself.

Many relationships, as in a family, are linked. What you do or say to one person can have an effect on any number of other people. This can make things more confusing and more interesting—therefore, honesty and transparency in all your relationships go a long way toward simplifying problems.

Living with and relating to teenagers can be particularly exasperating. A handy "how-to" guide is *Get Out of My Life, but First Could You Drive Me and Cheryl to the Mall?: A Parent's Guide to the New Teenager*, by Anthony E. Wolf, Ph.D.

Tough as any relationship may be, I believe that the lessons I learned and describe in this book can make any relationship work better. When my daughter was a teenager, she developed a modified form of the Miraculous Results Formula when asking for permission to do something. She had the habit of surprising me with last-minute requests to go here or do that. I would often say no simply because I didn't have time to check on the propriety and safety of her request. Then she learned to give me as much lead time as possible and to couch her request as something she would like to do rather than something she absolutely, positively had to do or her life would end. Now, I had the time to check with her mother to be sure she hadn't already nixed the idea and to make calls to other parents to ensure the presence of reliable adults. Since she didn't demand my agreement, it was easier for me to give it. This same technique works just as well between adults: my wife and I give each other a heads-up about what we would like to do in the near future, because it gives us each some time to think about it without feeling rushed.

One of the rewarding aspects of growing older and learning and practicing these techniques is that I am now just a little bit less clueless about what is going on with me and the people around me. I like being more comfortable in my relationships!

FIX YOURSELF

Between you and your partner, the only person you have legitimate control over is yourself. Learning how to show love to your partner and how to have constructive conversations are important parts of improving your relationship. There are, however, still other things you can do to improve yourself and make your relationship even better.

The advice that follows will help. But, if you are like me, nothing in this book will get you the whole way to a comfortable relationship. I started counseling as a gift to myself, before I knew how much I actually needed it. Even where professional help isn't necessary, it can speed up the process. I needed it to sort out my past and identify damaging behavior. I needed a twelve-step program to provide me with a simple program for living my life properly. I needed the help and support of many friends to teach me, mostly by example, how to do things better. I needed, in essence, to accept that I was a "Smart Man" who could use all of the help I could get.

You're Dumber Than You Think!

Everyone is dumber than he or she thinks. Each of us is limited in some fashion. All of us can benefit from outside help. The best source is close friendships with the people who know you best, who have your best interests at heart, and who can tell you the unpleasant things you need to hear. Some people call this "checking their universe." It is always a good idea to check your universe. It usually comes naturally, especially for minor decisions, but sometimes you need a reminder to do it for the important decisions, too.

For years I wasn't very good at checking my universe. I would do one lame-brained thing after another without getting any input from the people who could help me evaluate my decisions. Often my friends would cringe when they heard what I was intending to do. Sometimes they would speak up. Other times they wouldn't, since I hadn't asked for their opinion.

Take a friend's unsolicited advice as a blessing. It is difficult to know when to confront someone who hasn't asked for your opinion, because he or she will already have made a decision, and your comments will be seen as disapproval at a time when acceptance is expected. My friends have continued to like and love me after some particularly asinine decisions on my part, and I could have saved myself some grief if I had listened to them.

Even more important, everyone is constantly making mistakes—frequent little ones and occasional big ones. It is important to cut yourself some slack. You aren't perfect. No one is—that is only obtainable by God. And if you use God as your standard of performance for yourself, you are going to fall short, and you are going to annoy the people around you—particularly if you hold them to the same standard. Accept that you are human, accept that you will be making mistakes forever, and get off your own and other people's cases.

Resentments and Expectations

You can't have resentment without unmet expectations—if everything is going your way, you don't have anything to be resentful or upset about, right? And if you are like me, you often may not know what unmet expectation is causing your resentment. Moreover, even when you identify an unmet expectation, it may not be the right or only one affecting you, because many expectations are subconscious. They are just a part of how we believe the world should work. As a result, we don't think to question whether all our expectations are even reasonable.

The important thing to understand about a resentment is that it is yours, not your partner's or anyone else's. Until you act on your resentment nobody will know that you even have one. When you do act on it, things can get confusing. When acting on subconscious unmet expectations—often without your even knowing—the words you say, the actions you take, and your body language will be out of sync with the situation. What a quagmire. And to add insult to injury, your partner will often know that you are acting unreasonably, even though she may not know precisely why.

Therefore, when things aren't right, assume you have a part in the problem and look into yourself before sharing your anger with your partner. If you discover that your expectation is a reasonable one—and there are many reasonable expectations—then you can deal with the actual problem. Reasonable expectations are those that satisfy your reasonable needs and wants without impinging on anyone else. (For examples of reasonable expectations see the section, "Needs vs. Wants.")

Here's an example of an unreasonable expectation. In my first marriage I had the expectation, without my knowing it, that my wife would cook and clean and do everything for me just like my mother. My first wife was then an artist (she is now a psychologist) who would have been happier had I done all the chores myself. My expectation that she do more than half of them was dangerous to the relationship. Since that marriage, I have done my own laundry and other personal tasks, even when my wives volunteered.

Now I also do the dishes before Mary begins to wonder if I am going to get around to doing them at all. If I am reminded that it is trash night, I take it out right then, even though I hadn't forgotten and was going to get to it later. When I get a reminder, I choose to think of it as something loving I can do for my wife right now. I could feel nagged (resentful), but I choose not to think about other explanations that would cause me to feel bad about myself or her or us. I even thank her for the reminder.

There is no easy solution to the resentment problem. When your resentment presents itself through bad feelings, pissy words, or petty behavior, try to think of the things that happened recently that upset you because they didn't go your way. Somewhere connected to that event is almost certainly an unmet expectation. By paying attention, you can develop the ability to identify your expectations. Then you can share the reasonable ones with your partner. Those that are unreasonable can and should eventually be retired as worthless baggage.

The important point here is that you have to find a way to deal with your resentments yourself. Resist acting on them until you have identified the unmet expectation behind your resentment, and decided whether that expectation is reasonable. It hurts a relationship when you speak or act forcefully for the wrong reasons, in pursuit of the wrong goals.

Clean It Yourself or Shut Up

One way to create a bad day, or make a bad day worse, is to spot a chore that needs doing and bring it to your partner's attention rather than doing it yourself. For example, you might say, "Honey, the bathtub is dirty." She thinks in response, "Well, if you noticed it was dirty and it bothered you enough to comment on it, why didn't you clean it yourself? And furthermore, what makes you think if it's that dirty I haven't noticed it myself and would have done something about it if I had had the time?" And finally, she will conclude, "What a jerk I'm married to!"

Assume your partner is in the relationship to do the best she can for the two of you. In other words, grow up and stop treating your partner like you are a teenager and she is your mother (or you are the supervisor and she is the worker). So, if you are not going to do anything about it, keep your mouth shut. If you want to score some love points, do it yourself without being asked.

If there is a chore-related situation that annoys you, look at your own expectations. Which ones are creating your resentment? If you still can't resolve the issue yourself, discuss your feelings of annoyance with your partner using appropriate communication techniques. (See the section, "The Miraculous Results Formula.")

My favorite relationship *faux pas* was committed by a friend's soon-to-be-ex-husband. In addition to not helping clean the bathroom, he would complain about the deficiencies with her very-adequate cleaning. One day, to try to please him (and certainly above and beyond the call of duty) she spent hours cleaning the bathroom. When he looked at the results he couldn't find any problems for several minutes—until he finally happened to look up and said: "You didn't wash the ceiling."

Be Pleasant Doing Chores

I would rather not go to Costco. My wife prefers that I go with her. If I don't go she becomes mildly disappointed with me. If I go and act pissy, she will eventually pick up my mood; no one can remain cheerful in the presence of a grump. So I go, and remain as cheerful as possible. She appreciates my effort and I get to benefit from her good mood, which lasts longer than the unpleasantness of shopping. My point is that if you are going to do something, particularly something you don't want to do, resist the urge to inflict your negative feelings on your partner because you will only spread your misery around.

There are chores we hate, but which must be done. If you share your dislike of the chore, by word or body language, it will probably affect your partner's mood. She may have the ability to charge into unpleasant tasks without sharing her displeasure (my wife certainly does), so try to appreciate that quality and to do the same for her.

There are undoubtedly exceptions personal to each of us. I have one I don't understand and that may be unique to me. I can't go with my wife to a greenhouse to buy plants without becoming upset and unpleasant. My wife thinks my problem is stupid (a word she allows herself to use and which doesn't have any particular negative significance when applied to me), but over the years she has never seen me succeed.

Eventually, I got lucky solving the shopping-at-greenhouses problem. After many years, many meltdowns, and many discussions about why I always get upset in greenhouses, she said in frustration and with sadness, "Maybe you shouldn't go to greenhouses with me any more." I knew a golden apple when one was offered but I didn't gloat. I said, in all seriousness, "Okay, maybe you're right." The next spring when she asked me to go to the greenhouses again, I said that we had sort of decided that maybe it wasn't a good idea for me to go with her anymore and that I thought it was probably the right decision. I used quite a few imprecise, waffly-words in my response. I didn't want to come anywhere near sounding immature with a response like, "But you said I didn't have to anymore." Or even worse, "Hey, you blew it last year when you let me off the hook." Neither was going to help. She remembered very well what she had suggested and she regretted it. She also knew, in the back of her mind, that it is best for both of us although she wishes it weren't so. So do I.

Sex

Sex is one of a relationship's greatest joys. Sex is also the 800-pound gorilla in a relationship, because when there is a problem with sex you can't ignore it and it can beat you up badly. Even if it seems as though only one of you has a problem with sex, the problem really belongs to you both. It is something you do together and you will have to find a solution together.

The most important thing you both can do if you're having a sexual problem is talk, talk, talk, talk, and more talk. Don't blame, or shame, or be unnecessarily "right." Personally, I hate talking about sex problems. But I hate the "gorilla" sitting between my wife and me even more. So I talk. Occasionally, I have even been able to initiate the conversation. This has scored love points, although it didn't seem like it at the time.

If you have sex problems in your relationship, the rules and principles in this book are a harmless place to start, but you are going to have to look elsewhere for a complete solution. I have learned a lot about relationships, but this is one area where I still have a lot more to learn. Sex problems can have many causes: shyness, distrust, sexual trauma, unresolved anger, the list is endless. I know from experience that couples counseling can help. I recently found a book that can help: *Rekindling Desire, A Step-by-Step Program to Help Low-Sex and No-Sex Marriages* by Barry McCarthy, Ph.D. and Emily McCarthy. Don't let the title fool you. This book addresses almost every sex problem I have ever heard about.

The most important thing is to be willing to do the work with your partner. Do whatever it takes to solve a sex problem—just as you would with any other tough problem in a relationship.

A Nice Guy

Each of the suggestions in this book can be applied to dating, as well as every other relationship you have. Dating has its own additional, peculiar hopes and desires, as well as trials and tribulations, which I am not going to discuss in this book.

I did learn one important thing about dating, however, that is counterintuitive and not understood by many of the men I know. When a woman tells you that you are "a nice guy," what she is really telling you is that while she doesn't want to hurt your feelings, she is never, ever going to have sex with you. If you want her as a platonic friend, you may be in luck. If you want her as a romantic partner, it is not going to happen—and you should move on.

The most important thing when dating, however, is to just be yourself. You don't want a potential partner falling for someone you made up. Eventually you will get tired of pretending to be someone you are not. Your goal is to find a person you like who also likes you as you really are. Life will be so much easier and happier then.

If dating really does have you confused, a fun book that will help you sort it out is *A Fine Romance: The Passage of Courtship from Meeting to Marriage* by Judith Sills, Ph.D. Apparently, there really is a structured progression to serious dating.

Divorce

Tough as any relationship may be, I believe that the ideas I learned and describe in this book can make any relationship work better. Even if a relationship is ultimately a bad one, these techniques can help you to identify what is wrong and decide whether the problems can be fixed. Sometimes relationships come to an end. Unfortunately, I am somewhat of an expert on divorce and can speak from experience. I left many relationships not knowing why I was leaving; this was sad and confusing for me. And not only did I experience my own divorces, but I handled divorce cases for several years at the beginning of my legal career.

Divorce is a form of temporary insanity that can last for several years after the dissolution. During this time it is even more important to check your inner motivations for your decisions, *before* acting on them. It is also more important to check with your friends before making any big changes. Too many people try to create a new, permanent relationship too soon after a breakup, before they, and their new partner, know who they are, while there are still too many unresolved influences from the recently failed relationship. This isn't fair to anyone. Others abandon friends in anger for perceived complicity in the failure. And some commit the ultimate sin, which they will regret later, of fighting with their ex through their children.

If you have children, your contacts with your ex will be more frequent. Co-parenting to the greatest extent possible is best for your children and for your own sense of self-worth and pride—you want to feel that you are doing the proper thing. Your children aren't at fault for the divorce, and they will be hurting. Do everything you can for them, even if it means your ex "wins" some battles. Forget about her appearing to get the better of you if, in fact, it is your children who will be benefiting.

Fighting during divorce is common and may even be cathartic, but don't fight in the presence of your children. They have completely different feelings about each of you than you have about each other. If you are tempted to fight with your ex through your children, as in trashing her to them or complicating her life solely to get back at her, don't. If you do, you will be lower than pond scum.

Some men want to stay friends with their exes. This is a mistake. Trying to maintain a friendship while terminating a marriage sends conflicting messages on both a conscious and a subconscious level. It is a prescription for confusion and additional hurt feelings. Of course it is important to remain courteous toward your ex, particularly if you have children together, but any ideas of friendship are best postponed for at least several years. Relationships with your ex, like the other people you don't like but have to deal with, benefit from all the relationship techniques in this book. You won't be showing her romantic love, but you should communicate clearly, without suffering any of the pitfalls mentioned earlier. The techniques in this book can be used anywhere.

I hope you don't decide to divorce. At least not until you have tried most of the ideas in this book and still come to the conclusion that it is the only thing to do. What you learn about yourself, and how relationships work, while trying to save a marriage will help you in any future relationships. As you develop more confidence in your relationship skills you will find yourself more comfortable in your own skin and happier regardless of what happens.

There is no easy way to split up, but there is a right way. The right way is to be as clear and honest with your soon-to-be-ex-partner as possible so that she understands why you are leaving. It isn't fair to yourself to leave until you know why you are doing so, and once you do understand why, it isn't fair to keep the reasons to yourself.

HELP YOUR PARTNER

Once you learn to show your love, communicate about problems, and fix yourself first, there is still plenty more you can do—and now you have the tools to do it well. The following sections offer additional ideas on how to make your partner's life better. That is the goal—making your partner's life better. I have found the task to be both wonderful and counterintuitive: the more I do to make my partner happy, the happier I become.

Bad Presents

There is one kind of action that women everywhere receive poorly—a practical present. Do not give a practical present. Only give a practical present if it is your partner's idea (and you did not even hint at it in the slightest). Require that your arm be twisted. Agree reluctantly and indicate you don't want to make a habit of practical presents—except for yourself, of course. With an impractical gift you may ring the bell and earn a love point, or not. But a practical gift, even if needed and expensive, will rarely be appreciated as a gift.

This is because providing the practical things necessary for maintaining a household is a normal, expected part of a relationship. Providing them shows love and will be appreciated. You will earn love points, but only if those practical things are not presented as gifts. People like to know they are special, and when you only give them something that must be provided anyway you are cheating them, and they will know it.

It's also a bad idea to give a gift that covers more than one holiday or anniversary. Even if two events occur on the same day you'd be wise to give two gifts. Don't shortchange your partner just because she happens to have been born on Christmas. Late presents are a mistake, too. The only time my mother ever yelled at me with real anger was a Christmas I returned home without presents.

There is an even bigger mistake you can make, though—worse than a bad present or a late present. That mistake is giving no present at all. My father committed it and got away with it, but he paid a price. A good friend of mine did it and lost his marriage.

Start thinking of gifts for holidays and anniversaries in a new way. These should be gifts that demonstrate you are paying attention and that your regard for your partner extends beyond necessities of life. I listen to my wife for clues as to things she might like and keep an eye out for things that might please her. I keep a gift or two in reserve. As I write this I have a necklace hidden away. She saw it in a store and liked it but decided not to buy it. When my wife wasn't looking I signaled the salesperson to set it aside. I went back the next day and bought it. My wife will get it for her birthday long before you read this book, and by then I will have something else in reserve.

Some of the gifts I have given her have not been to her liking, but she appreciates the thought and the time it took to buy it for her. That's because the gifts are given out of love—and sometimes, I really do give her a gift for no other reason than to show her this love. No holiday, no anniversary, just love. The first time I did this was when I first mentioned to her that I kept presents in reserve. She thought I was joking, so I got up and gave her one. It was earrings that matched a ring I had already given her. It made one hell of an impression! Now that I think of it, that might have been a loving action that created an impression stronger than a single love point. It showed my wife that I was actively working on ways to show my love for her beyond what she had expected or thought possible. That one really worked well for both of us.

Being in a relationship requires adherence to the social norms so that your partner knows that you are paying attention to the relationship. Don't shrug off the standard and traditional social, holiday, and rites-of-passage expectations—even if you believe that Valentine's Day was invented by chocolate-makers and greeting card companies to make a profit.

A last word here. Giving flowers is a special way to show love. Women seem to have more of an affinity for flowers than men. I don't know why that is. I like to think that in addition to the beauty of flowers, the very fact of their impermanence is important. The impermanence of the gift is a statement that you are dealing with your partner in the here-and-now. As you keep giving impermanent flowers, it is a demonstration that you are going to continue to replace them and continue to love her.

Needs vs. Wants

Needs are the things in life you can't live comfortably without; food, water, and clothing are obvious examples. Every person has similar obvious *needs* that keep life and limb together. *Wants* are the things you would like to have but your life won't be much worse if you never get them.

Problems arise when the two are confused. Certain things that are *wants* for one person may be a *need* for another. My wife, frugal as she is, has a *need* for good bedding to feel that she is a success. I have a *need* to trek in Nepal to feel that I am a success. Other people don't care one way or the other about these things, but to my wife and me, each is very important to how we feel about ourselves, and to how successful we feel in the world.

It is important to learn which of the things that are *wants* for most people are actually *needs* for your partner. Then it is important to help her get them. Equally important is to know what your own *needs* are that are only *wants* for most other people. This is an important part of figuring out what is negotiable in your relationship, and what shouldn't be compromised lest your personal hopes and dreams suffer. You can't compromise on needs without potentially doing damage to yourself and your relationship.

It is important to remember that there are many things (needs, expectations) that are very important to you that your partner may not care about or even think about. She may act in ways that confuse or hurt you solely because she doesn't understand that your desire, inconsequential to her, is crucial to you. Conversely you may be annoying her without intending to by being fervently involved in something that seems trivial to her.

Let your partner know what your needs are so that she doesn't inadvertently hurt you by keeping you from them. When you identify your needs, you allow your partner to understand that you are not being selfish about something that appears unimportant to her. You also give her the opportunity to help you achieve those needs—and you, of course, have the same obligation to her.

Sometimes, because that's the way life works, each of you will have to compromise on your needs, but when you do, you and your partner will understand the importance of what is being given up. If all is going well, you will have a sympathetic partner to offer consolation.

Keep in mind that having children is more often a need than a want.

Reaffirm Your Partner

Avoid random, pointless comments that diminish what your partner says. Nobody likes a spoilsport. Much of what people say is just idle commentary about the day, dreams they have, and things they would like to do.

My wife has said that she would love to spend a vacation with me in Paris. I don't say that I don't like big cities in Europe, which is true, or that the exchange rate would kill us, which is also true. I say, "Wouldn't that be nice." I haven't committed myself, and I haven't burst her dream. When she says that some politician is a real jerk, I say, "I know what you mean." I haven't endorsed her feeling about him but I have acknowledged her feelings. When she says that we are going to have to fix the water-stained wall in the living room someday, I just grimace and nod to let her know that I have heard her and that it is going to be a real pain-in-the-ass job.

In any of these instances, and an infinite number of similar situations, if I start to talk about practicalities or my own preferences, I have changed her casual musings into a more serious discussion. She isn't looking for a serious discussion. (She has proven she knows how to have one when she chooses.) She is just wishing and dreaming and hoping and venting, and in the process, she is also letting me know that she loves me and would like to experience some more of her dreams with me.

I, too, share my dreams, both big and small, in casual conversation with her all the time. I would love to go trekking in Nepal again. I've already gone once on my own and once with her. She knows how much I love it and she knows it will take effort to go a third time, but she lets me dream about it out loud over and over again. And if it works out we will go back to Nepal, and I will go to Paris, and it will be "A Perfect Vacation."

A Perfect Vacation

A perfect vacation for your partner is a way to show love that can transcend the short shelf life of most loving actions. If you remember that your only goal is to make it perfect for her, it can be a lot of fun for you, too. I got the idea from a friend who had just come back from visiting her mother. Her mother smokes and my friend hates smoking. My friend said that since she wanted to mend her relationship with her mother she didn't comment on her smoking once during her three-day visit. She said that she and her mother got along better than they had in years.

It was a lesson I really needed to learn. During my first marriage, my wife and I took a two-week vacation to visit my parents in Santa Barbara—two full weeks. The only thing my wife said she wanted to do was go to the beach. I had hundreds of things I wanted to do and each time we headed for the beach we would pass one or more of them and get distracted. Two full weeks and I got her to the beach for forty-five minutes on an overcast day. There is a picture of us on that beach, and nobody is smiling. I had to learn to do better.

When my daughter was fourteen I took her to Seattle for a five-day vacation of shopping, eating, and playing—anything and everything she wanted to do. We stayed in a hotel at the Pike Street Market where things are always happening. We ate where she wanted. We shopped for school clothes and special clothes for her. We went to a movie at 1 a.m. We took a ferry ride. She was in charge of what we did the entire time. I never had to decide what to do. If she ran out of ideas I would offer suggestions, since I knew the city and she didn't. But she always got to decide. She has never forgotten the great time we had.

Once you decide that a particular vacation or a particular day is going to be solely for your partner (or daughter, or friend), figuring out how to do it becomes part of the fun. You won't feel cheated because you will be doing exactly what you want to do, which is to make your partner feel great.

Do not advertise your intention to your partner. By saying that you are doing this just for her, you create both an obligation for her to feel she "must" have fun and an obligation to reciprocate. The suggestion should appear spontaneous, as in "Why don't we…" or, "I think I would like to…" knowing full well your suggestion is actually what she would like to do. Sometimes all you have to do is agree with her own idea, and then focus on making it great for her.

If you don't know what she would like to do, you haven't been paying enough attention to her. Start paying attention or start asking questions. As I write this I realize that I have missed some blatant hints from my wife: she would love nothing better than to go to New York City and see some Broadway plays.

The Gift of Success

When my wife and I got married we bought a new mattress. I had been living on a hard-as-a-rock futon, and her mattress sagged like an old horse. When we began shopping for a mattress it soon became clear that we weren't even remotely on the same page. I was looking in Costco in the substantially-under-one-thousand-dollar range and she was taking me into stores I didn't know existed and then heading for the most expensive mattress sets there. I kept resisting and she kept persisting.

What she wanted was a mattress and box springs priced at thirty-five hundred dollars but marked down to twenty-two hundred. At that time we were sharing living expenses fifty-fifty and I thought that even my half of the reduced price was nuts. My wife is usually quite frugal and her behavior was confusing to me.

But I was listening and what I eventually heard over the next several days, without her ever actually saying it, was that one of the ways she measured the success of her life was by the quality of her bed and bedding. Bingo! There was no way I could spend over a thousand dollars for my share of a mattress, but I would happily spend many times that amount to help my wife feel that she was a success. All it took was an attitude change based on what I really wanted to accomplish. And here's a plus: all my life I had been awakened at night with bad knee pain. It hasn't happened once in the decade since we got that mattress.

When I am lucky enough to learn that my wife wants something specific for a gift, I go out of my way to get it for her. I did the same for my daughter, sometimes against the wishes of her stepmothers. When she desperately wanted a porce faced teddy bear or a brass-and-crystal fairy wand that were within our budget, but deemed by my partner too silly, I got them anyway. Who cares how silly they are when the person you love really, really wants them? You can only show your love for someone when it is done in a way that she will notice and accept. My wife's piano cost more than she thought she could afford—but I knew her price range and I offered the difference so that she could get the piano she wanted.

To hell with worrying about silly and impractical when love is involved and happiness is yours to grant.

What If It Isn't Broken?

Fix it anyway! I can't emphasize this enough. Fix it anyway! Work on your relationship all the time. Your partner deserves your continuing efforts to make the relationship better still. Relationship maintenance and the related improvements are normal. The process is not that different from pursuing a hobby or a sport, or maintaining a car or boat. We men typically work on and maintain our possessions, right? We practice to improve our performance in the sports and activities we enjoy. We can and should put at least the same energy into our relationship with our partner. I know from experience that a well-cared-for wife is a joy and well worth the investment.

Don't become complacent when things are going well, because outside forces will intervene, perfection will slip away, and time will change everything, just as often for the worse. What was perfect at one time may not stay perfect for all time. Always pay attention to the relationship because several times a decade, adults enter new stages in their emotional and mental makeup that changes the way they think and feel about things. The changes are subtler than the changes from adolescent to teenager, or teenager to young adult, but they do exist. The adult changes are often so subtle that it can take a while to know that they have happened. But when they do happen, your partner could well have a new set of attitudes and feelings for no other reason than that she has entered the next stage of adulthood.

This means that several times a decade you are going to have to relearn how to interact with a partner who is now different from the one you knew so well. If you have developed the habit of constantly and continuously fine-tuning your relationship with her, you will be able to automatically adjust as these changes happen.

You may sense that something is out of sorts or different with the world or your partner. What worked before doesn't work now. What was okay then isn't okay now. Remember, though, you are changing just as often. Since you are also going through your own changes it is almost impossible to tell when the differences that you think you notice in others are actually changes in you. An accusation that the other person has changed is just as likely to be wrong as right. It could just as easily be you who has changed.

Multiply two people times two changes per decade, and you get four changes per decade. It happens slowly and it is going on with one or the other of you almost all the time. You rarely know if it is you or your partner who is changing, although it will always seem to be her. If, however, you are already constantly, consciously working to improve your relationship, you will be able to accommodate every change, both hers and yours, with little extra effort.

Important Rites of Passage

Engagement rings, weddings, wedding anniversaries, birthdays, children's births, and other celebrations are exceptions to the rule that all love points are the same size. There are times when you are expected to participate in cultural rites of passage and are expected to participate in the proper way. Take my word for it: You fail to do so at your peril! The love points are only somewhat bigger for these kinds of events, but failing to earn these particular points will create a lifelong negative memory for your partner. Assume that the events and rituals, particularly those surrounding marriage and having children, are very important to her no matter how they seem to you. I learned this the hard way.

When my first wife was pregnant with our daughter and it was time to prepare our home for her, I joked that since the baby would be too little to tell the difference, we could even keep her in a cardboard box for the first few months. My intent, I think, was to indicate that I didn't want to spend a lot of money on a bassinet that would only be used for several months. I should have kept my mouth shut. With that one comment I sent a message to my wife that I wasn't as excited about having a child as she was, that I wasn't willing to do everything I could for our child, and that I wasn't going to participate as a parent to the extent she had hoped—a complete trifecta of disaster. My mistake may seem obvious to you, but it wasn't to me at the time.

Everybody has blind spots, so paying a little extra attention in certain situations can pay big dividends. My third wife sought me out just before our wedding ceremony and handed me an expensive, solid gold money clip as a pre-wedding ceremony gift. I had never even heard of such a gift, and I had already been married twice before!—and I had no gift for her. Her smile became rigid, her shoulders fell, she sighed, and off we went to get married.

Sometimes you are going to be ambushed by your partner's unvoiced and therefore unknown expectations, no matter how good your intentions. Nailing the ones you do know about will help smooth over your lapses. It is safest to consider that the traditions and ceremonies that surround engagements, weddings, having children, and even birthdays, have virtually nothing to do with you. Assume that they are all about your partner, her expectations, and the rites of passage that are important to her. What you need to do in each of these situations is find out what is expected of you. Then do it without the slightest indication of resistance, dissent, or complaint. These events are integral to a woman's sense of all being right with the world and having life turn out the way she always thought it should. If you don't get these events right, your shortcomings will become a negative memory for your partner that can never be erased. By my fourth wedding I finally got everything right—my wife still glows with the memories. Find out what your partner expects around all these rite-of-passage events.

I recommend always deferring to your bride's choices unless you have a strong feeling about how something should be done. Don't object merely because what she wants seems silly or unnecessary to you. Weddings are formalized public functions that follow certain rules. If they didn't matter to either of you, you could get married at the courthouse. Weddings are much nicer.

I believe, however, that it is okay to voice your feelings if you are concerned about the total expense of the wedding. It would be dishonest not to share concerns that affect you materially. But with anything you don't feel very strongly about, let your bride have her way. If you do feel strongly, and have supporting reasons that make sense to you and others, only then you should speak. In this situation I recommend that you first check what you want to say with a disinterested friend before opening your mouth.

• • •

Your partner isn't the only one whose expectations need to be considered. There are also women (and occasionally men) in each family who may have conflicting ideas about how your wedding should go. Don't get drawn into choosing one family's ideas over the other. You always want to be on your bride's side. If you feel cornered tell them, "I want my bride to have this wedding go exactly the way she wants. I'll go ask her what she would like and get back to you."

Commitment

The decision to help your partner is the cornerstone of commitment. Some people "make" commitments. I am lousy at making important commitments, but I am excellent at keeping the ones I discover I have. It does me no good to try to create a commitment. I spend my time checking to see if I already have one. I don't worry about the rest. For me, a commitment is like a belief—I either have it or I don't. When I do have a commitment, it rings true to me and to the people around me. The last time I spoke with my mother-in-law she was slumped in a chair in a nursing home, unable to speak or even raise her head to nod. I knelt next to her, explained my personal belief about commitment, and told her that I had discovered that I was committed to her daughter. Because of my commitment, I would take care of her daughter to the best of my ability for the rest of my life. She got the message. When I left she had tears running down her cheeks.

When we got married, my wife's best friend, who is a tough Teamster Business Agent, gave her away. On our way in to the ceremony he sought me out and put his arm around my shoulder. I thought he was going to congratulate me, which he did, but he also said: "If this doesn't work, Kelly, I'm going to break both of your knees." I'm pretty sure he was kidding, but it didn't matter. I knew I was doing the right thing and that the marriage would be a success. I said, "Michael, if this doesn't work, you have my permission to break my knees." We understood each other.

No matter how you discover or create a commitment, you need to act on it the same way you do when showing love. They are done the same way. It is the day in and day out consistency of paying attention discussed in previous chapters that does it. If you don't, your partner will doubt that you have a commitment to her.

When my wife is feeling insecure, she asks again that I never leave her. I say I never will and it rings true to both of us because it is a commitment that I have and that I demonstrate in all the things I do for her and for us.

LIFE IS GOOD

Don't think of all the rules for showing love as tasks to be accomplished and checked off a list. You won't have any fun doing that. Practice them until they become second nature. If you have difficulty finding your stride, consider changing your attitude. It is not impossible to do. The following chapters show attitude shifts I have made. With luck, you should be able to figure out how to make some of your own.

Good Luck

I have been lucky my entire life. Even the things that I thought were disasters at the time (including three failed marriages!) usually turned out to benefit me in the long run. Some people have resented my luck—and I too once wondered if my luck was deserved. But rejecting it doesn't help anyone else. I would be irresponsible to not take advantage of it, because those bits of luck that have given me a better education, better health, and greater opportunities have benefited my family, my friends, and myself. Increased ability and opportunity creates increased responsibility. When I ask, "Which of God's graces would I deny?" the only appropriate answer I can come up with is, "None of them!" I'm not smart enough to know what God's grand scheme is, so it seems foolish to reject a gift from God.

Accept good luck when it comes your way, gladly and without guilt. It is not a matter of whether you deserve it or not. You aren't competent to judge that. No one is. It is a gift. And the only appropriate response to the receipt of a gift is to accept it, say thank you, and use it appropriately.

Perfection Is Relative

I believe my wife is perfect for me. She isn't perfect, of course. She is as far from perfect as anyone else. But I have decided to accept that her imperfections are, somehow, in my best interest—she is perfect for me. But even on a straight benefit–deficit analysis, without considering any redeeming elements for her deficiencies, she is still the best partner I have ever found.

I have come to believe that I am a lousy judge of what is good for me. Many of the events in my life that I thought were disasters turned out to be beneficial in hindsight. My third marriage, tough as it was, taught me that I had developed good relationship skills. The army convinced me that I wanted to go back to college. Drinking too much showed me that I wanted to become a better person.

At times Mary thinks she is too bitchy and nags me too much. Fortunately for her, one of my previous wives was better at nagging, and I hardly notice. If she is bitchy or nagging about something unimportant to me, it doesn't have any emotional bite. If, however, the nagging relates to a legitimate concern on her part, and I can do something to make her feel better or more secure, then I pay attention and do what I can.

I have made a conscious decision to focus on the silver lining of every negative situation. With practice this has become a habit, my default position. You can do the same, especially if you are ready to let go of being right. Many people think the "right" response to a negative situation is gloom and doom. But once you acknowledge what has happened, there is no harm in focusing on the positive. The negative event is in the past. Why not focus on the future's positive possibilities?

Here's an example. I grew up in a giant house. My physical needs were well met. I had plenty of vacations and adventures. I was sent to a prep school for a great education. Yet in spite of all of this, for some unknown reason, I thought I had had a bad childhood. This belief kept me unhappier than I needed to be into my adult life. When I complained about my childhood, people thought I was nuts. Then one day, for no apparent reason, as I was sitting at a red light, I realized that I had had a wonderful childhood. I was a bit gloomy as a child, but my childhood had actually been fine. I don't know what caused me to change my attitude at that particular time— my childhood didn't change, because it was already over and done with, but my attitude about it changed and that made all the difference.

That change in attitude about my childhood was a gift. Other changes in attitude have been the result of long hard work. In every instance I was the thing that had to change, and I am happier for the changes.

Assume the Best

Adopt the habit of assuming the best in any situation that is not obviously negative. Many people automatically assume that there is negative intent in every unfavorable situation. Not me. Not anymore. I have turned the assumption of goodness, or at most inattention, into my default position. Every day we get to decide how we feel about the things that happen to us. Too often that decision happens in our subconscious. It doesn't have to stay that way.

Once I parked in a legal spot, on a Sunday afternoon, on an unoccupied street, in a quiet part of town. I came out and found a parking ticket on my car. I just paid it without a fight. The situation was so absurd that the only thing I could think of was that the cop who gave me the ticket was having a monumentally bad day and that by writing that ticket he was able to let off enough steam so that when he went home he didn't have to beat his wife and kids. It was my small contribution to domestic peace that day.

I used to get pissed off when someone cut me off in traffic without signaling. Now, instead, I think about the bell curve and human intelligence. Human intelligence is distributed unevenly throughout humanity. The distribution can be described with a bell curve. Most people are of average intelligence. Some are more intelligent than average and some are less intelligent than average. Since I understand the bell curve distribution but have no knowledge of the actual numbers, I assume that three-fifths of people are of about average intelligence, one-fifth are above average in intelligence, and one-fifth are below average in intelligence. That means that one in every five drivers I encounter on the road is operating with below-average intelligence!

Now, for instance, when I see someone fail to signal I give them more room and silently thank them for concentrating their limited mental abilities on the more important driving functions like keeping their car on the road and not running into other people—important tasks which they might forget to do if they overloaded their limited mental capabilities by attempting to signal too.

And even in Lake Woebegone, where everyone is above average, or will be when they grow up, people are going to have bad days and not pay adequate attention to their driving or anything else they may be doing or saying. It is usually obvious when someone is having a bad day and is consciously or unconsciously taking it out on the people around him or her. I feel that person's bad day is usually punishment enough for him or her. I just give that individual a wide berth.

Am I right about the bad drivers and the vindictive cop? I have no idea. But I do know that they do not bother me anymore. Am I ignoring reality? Well, yes and no. I may be wrong about the objective world that is constantly presenting me with challenges, but my internal reality is what I think it is and how I feel about it. I have an obligation to myself to improve my inner reality whenever possible.

I choose to think that all the typical annoyances I encounter repeatedly throughout the day are unintentional, inadvertent, and not directed specifically at me, unless there is evidence to the contrary.

I do the same thing in my relationships. I assume no malice unless the assumption is unavoidable. I accept that my partner is a typically flawed human and I assume that she loves me. Because I have been wrong about my life and people's intentions so often, the only sane thing for me to do is believe that everything is fine, in spite of my tendency to think otherwise, unless I have some hard facts that prove otherwise.

Wife Whisperer

When my wife says to me, "You're the best," I respond, "Second best." When she asks if I am happy, I tell her that it would take two of me to be any happier. When she has been bitchy and is worried about my reaction, I tell her that I barely noticed and that anyway she is a lightweight at being bitchy. When she becomes over-concerned about some relatively minor problem I agree and suggest that whoever is responsible deserves to be nuked. She laughs because she knows that I have been paying attention to her, which is more important to her happiness than whatever the problem is. Then, she usually sees that she has overreacted to the situation and nuking won't really be necessary.

Once you have developed the habit of sharing all your positive thoughts, you can expand your repertoire with more loving, playful, even teasing responses that you create on the fly. Continue to make your love obvious by responding with a positive spin on whatever your partner has just said. When Mary and I first started dating she called some of her old flames to tell them it was time to give up. She truly is a unique woman and one of them asked, "How is he liking his visit to Mary Ruckerland?" (Rucker is her maiden name.) After Mary told me about his comment, I had a passport stamp made for "Mary Ruckerland" and gave it to her for Christmas. You don't need to get fancy—just get creative.

At the end of the day, it's simple. Just keep showing your partner that you are paying attention and that you love her. That is all it takes.

MARY RUCKERLAND
ENTRY PERMIT
KF APR 0 7 1995 93
(Bona Fide Visitor)
DEPARTMENT OF IMMIGRATION

THE END? HARDLY!

Remember the old saying that a journey of many miles begins with a single step? It has two meanings. The obvious one is that every journey is accomplished in successive, discrete steps. The less obvious one is that once you realize there is a need for the journey, you can't stay where you are; you have to take that first step.

The end of this book is really just the beginning for you. You decided to read this book, and you did it for a reason. Now you are committed to doing something—eventually. Why not now? You can't go back to ignorance. Nor can you stay the same as you were and do nothing, knowing there are ways to improve your relationship.

But remember, when things start to get better in your relationship, they may appear to be getting worse for a while. This is because you will be operating out of your comfort zone until you discover how these new rules and principles work, and until they become habits. I have been told that new habits usually take at least three weeks to become second nature—so don't get discouraged and quit before the three weeks are up.

And as you work at the new behavior, it may raise your partner's expectations and she may want to see even more improvement. Try to think of it this way, though: If she thinks that you should be doing still more, you must now be on the right track and succeeding. Just keep plugging away until it gets easy. A smart woman will give you time to work on your behavior, and let you improve at your own speed.

We can't improve alone. I learned everything I know about relationships from other people. With their help I have been able to reach my goal of being at least as sane as the average person in relationships. To all those who helped me, I say, "I'm better now, thank you." I hope you will be as successful.

And besides, what else are you going to do with your time? Here's what:

Don't make your partner a part of your perfect world; instead, work to make your partner's world perfect.

You will be happier in the long run.

ACKNOWLEDGEMENTS

I have spent my entire life accepting help, and writing this book was no exception. Allen Blair, Caroline Blair, Rod Bradley, Don Edwards, Holly Fisher, John Fisher, Mary Fisher, Carmen Gutierrez, Tawana Jolin, Susan LaGrande, Jan Lindeman, Karen Russell, Nancy Shaw, Jack Sterne, and Michelle Stone all provided suggestions that helped turn my jumble of ideas into a coherent book. And then my editor, Sarah Cypher, made it readable. The book's deficiencies are because I rejected too much of their good advice.

Purchase copies of this book at:
www.acluelessman.com